Stay Young with T'ai Chi

Flexible, Mobile,
and Stress Free—After 50

Ellae Elinwood

TUTTLE PUBLISHING
Boston · Rutland, Vermont · Tokyo

613.7148

First published in 2004 by Tuttle Publishing, an imprint of Periplus Editions (HK) Ltd., with editorial offices at 153 Milk Street, Boston, Massachusetts 02109.

Library of Congress Cataloging-in-Publication Data

Elinwood, Ellae.
  Stay young with t'ai chi : flexible, mobile, and stress free-after 50
/ Ellae Elinwood.-- 1st ed.
      p. cm.
Includes bibliographical references.
  ISBN 0-8048-3498-9 (pbk.)
  1. Tai chi--Therapeutic use. 2. Health. I. Title. RM727.T34E43 2004
613.7'148--dc22
                              2003026588

Distributed by

North America, Latin America
and Europe
Tuttle Publishing
Distribution Center
Airport Industrial Park
364 Innovation Drive
North Clarendon, VT
05759-9436
Tel: (802) 773-8930
Fax: (802) 773-6993
info@tuttlepublishing.com
www.tuttlepublishing.com

Japan
Tuttle Publishing
Yaekari Building, 3rd Floor
5-4-12 Osaki
Shinagawa-ku
Tokyo 141 0032
Tel: (03) 5437-0171
Fax: (03) 5437-0755
tuttle-sales@gol.com

Asia Pacific
Berkeley Books Pte. Ltd.
130 Joo Seng Road
#06-01/03 Olivine Building
Singapore 368357
Tel: (65) 6280-1330
Fax: (65) 6280-6290
inquiries@periplus.com.sg

First edition
08 07 06 05 04   10 9 8 7 6 5 4 3 2 1

Printed in the United States of America

Contents

Dedication

To those who have gone before us, specifically Jou, Tsung Hwa, master of T'ai Chi and author of *The Tao of T'ai Chi Ch'uan, Way to Rejuvenation*, without which this book could not have been written.

Foreword

I love growing old. The headlong hormones of youth, though deliriously enjoyable while they lasted, seem graciously and gratefully replaced by a longer sense of time and a deeper appreciation of the beautiful in the ordinary—I love the unique and ever-changing view of trees, light, and sky out of my bedroom window as I wake each morning. There seems to be more time to breathe, look, and listen. As I grow older I sense a subtle sinking into the core of life where things, people, ideas, and thoughts flow a bit more smoothly than in my youth and this flow becomes a most interesting dance.

T'ai Chi has been my dance for the past fifteen years, and, like life, it is both the same and different every day and it is always a mystery. T'ai Chi is like a lovely handcrafted bowl or cup which can hold anything within its empty form: tea, rice, refuse, roses, coffee, vodka, veggies, meat, oil, or dirt. . . . And it holds all of these things without judgment or fear. Likewise, the form of T'ai Chi can, and has, held everything I've brought to it over these many years: joy, fear, disappointment, anger, sorrow, ecstasy, pain, delight, wonder. . . . It has cradled these emotions without judgment and has given back support and grace.

T'ai Chi has never let me down. I always feel "good" after doing T'ai Chi—there are never any regrets.

Though a martial art, T'ai Chi is also a moving meditation, and as such, its practice helps me etch out a few moments of relaxed awareness in my rather busy schedule—a necessary and welcomed balance to meetings, rehearsals, recording sessions, classes, practice, and composing. Not only can T'ai Chi hold and transform any emotion or energy that you bring to it, it can also "be" anything you may want it to be: a meditation, a martial art, a playground, a dance, a journey, an exercise, a healing, a break, a silence.

Ellae's delightful and caring presentation of the essence of T'ai Chi and Qigong practice and philosophy is a joy to read and to practice. Through her clear descriptions you can be practicing within moments, and remember that it only takes a few moments of daily practice to begin to accumulate a deep well of relaxation and a storehouse of vital energy.

Stop, look, listen, breathe, and enjoy practicing T'ai Chi and Qigong!

—Todd Barton

Todd Barton is resident Composer and Music Director of the Oregon Shakespeare Festival; Director of Composition Studies for the Music Department at Southern Oregon University; Composer of Genome Music. See his web site at www.toddbarton.com.

Introduction: You and T'ai Chi

Welcome. You have begun an exploration into a movement phenomenon that has very rapidly spread throughout the world. T'ai Chi, a Chinese health system and exercise that promotes well-being, and longevity, has been exquisitely cultivated over the last 2,500 years. However, it is only in the past fifty years that T'ai Chi has traveled from its birthplace among the people of China to the West. Today, diligent and devoted students of all races, creeds, colors, and faiths have joined in receiving the benefits that have long been associated with a profound ability to improve the quality of health and well-being for any committed practitioner.

What is Tai Chi?

T'ai Chi (T'ai is pronounced TIE and Chi is pronounced CHEE) is derived from the martial art *T'ai Chi Ch'uan*, of which there are three basic forms: *Chen*, *Wu*, and *Yang*. Chen style is noted for its fast and explosive movements. Wu style expresses soft, yet fully formed movements. Yang has evolved into the T'ai Chi that we are most familiar with and that is arguably the most popular form of T'ai Chi Ch'uan in our Western world. The Yang form is made up of smooth, flowing movements that emphasize the grace of T'ai Chi. This is the form that will be taught in this book.

T'ai Chi is a series of movements done in a predictable, flowing sequence that gently stretch and tone every muscle in our body and dramatically improve the balance and overall functioning of our joints and organs. T'ai Chi's primary purpose is to enhance the accumulation and storage of *chi*, which is believed by many to be *the* vital force of life—the source of liveliness that surrounds and permeates all living things. It is from chi that we receive the essence of life and our liveliness, and it is the ability to keep an accurate, flowing balance within our body that dictates our personal level of health and well-being. Through T'ai Chi movements the body becomes more receptive to chi and becomes better able to use this vitality to create optimum health.

From your own practice in T'ai Chi, you will notice two basic areas of our health that T'ai Chi affects: the physiological—the body—and the psychological—the mind and emotions. Here's a quick look at the benefits of each.

The Physiological Benefits

T'ai Chi positions incorporate all of the body's muscles through movements that use each muscle group exactly as they were naturally set up to be used. Every position brings a specific muscle into action and then relaxes it when the action is complete, allowing your muscles to be toned in a natural balance with one another. Stretch, relax, stretch, relax—you will be working your body as it was designed to be used. Injury-free, coordinated action, and grace of movement merge to facilitate the T'ai Chi benefits.

The results of research that has been undertaken so far indicate that T'ai Chi affects muscle tone, coordination, balance, posture, breathing, joint flexibility, mobility, blood pressure, migraines, and even skin tone. This one form of exercise accomplishes so much and is so safe that it is virtually impossible to hurt yourself while actually doing T'ai Chi (unless you slip on a loose rug!).

As often happens, one thing leads to another. As your muscles are toned, your coordination becomes easier. Your new and improved coordination will assure better balance. When balanced, posture is easier to correct. As your posture opens, your lungs expand and breathing becomes easier. As your breath creates more oxygen the joints will be under less stress and mobility will naturally improve. As you reduce stress your blood pressure will respond by becoming more stable. Your headaches will reduce and your skin, reaping the benefits of breath, blood, and ease of movement, will start to glow. You will probably even see your weight stabilize.

This wonderful energizing relationship to your body is taught through the movements themselves. The act of moving into the predictable sequenced motions also creates the understanding of what it means to relax within the form. As you continue your experience you will be encouraged to let the lower half of your body, from the waist down, become very stable. It is a feeling of letting the weight throughout the upper body all settle down below the waist. In contrast you let your upper body— torso, arms, and shoulders—lighten up. To increase this feeling of lightness, you move as though your head is suspended from a string emerging from the crown. Duplicating these ideas into your life and practice starts you on your first step toward the great physical benefits T'ai Chi offers.

This building toward health is a process that soundly incorporates the Eastern concept of strength. Different from our Western belief that strength is hard, held in, tough, and capable of lifting great burdens, the Chinese definition

Possible Physiological Benefits

Increased joint flexibility
Increased mobility
Improved muscle tone
Improved breath capacity
Improved circulation
Improved ease of movement
Improved balance
Balanced blood pressure
Reduced carpal-tunnel syndrome
Greater ease walking
Greater ease lifting and directing
   your feet
Reduction in girth

Possible Psychological Effects

Reduction of stress
Reduction of anxiety
Reduction of depression
Balances moods
Improves ability to focus and
   concentrate
Decreased dependency on
   substances
Improved weight and height ratio
Improved pleasure in life

Be Empty
Empty of thoughts
Empty of expectations
Empty of performance
Empty of anxiety
Empty of comparison
Empty of competition

of strength embraces toned and supple muscles that are relaxed to the touch but able to mobilize with lightning speed when action is required. When a muscle is held "strong" all the time it is using valuable energy, or chi, to maintain that constant holding. Always mobilized for action but perhaps seldom actually moving is hugely inefficient. You may feel this is not a problem, but check your shoulder muscles. Are they soft and pliable or tough and hard? Does your back bother you? Is your neck tight, stiff, or sore? All these and more are outcomes of "strong" muscles no longer elastic, actually having lost their natural tone. And discomfort, whether minor or a real pain, is a predictable outcome.

T'ai Chi trains your body to let go of all this unnecessary holding, thus freeing up the chi in that area to flow more freely throughout the body. After practicing regularly, your muscles will arrive at a state of balanced elasticity and your chi will be freed to assist your health and your improved sense of well-being.

A toned body that is strong as an ox, as supple as a tiger, and as quick as a striking snake requires a type of strength that is much more complex than just power lifting. To acquire this type of strength requires gaining skills of strength, agility, grace, relaxation, readiness, effective breathing, and confident movement. T'ai Chi's simple movements provide all that is needed to retain these qualities for yourself. These qualities demand the efficient use of one's personal energy. The easy energy of youth is now less available, so learning T'ai Chi's wise methods of efficient use of body energies makes great and good sense.

It usually takes about six weeks of practice to experience the very beginnings of change. Then in six months' time the changes will be well in place and progressing nicely. These results, of course, depend completely on how faithfully you engage in your practices. The more you incorporate the T'ai Chi life warmups into your daily events and devote yourself to practice, the more profoundly you will experience the offerings T'ai Chi brings to you.

The Psychological Benefits

Chi is the key to well-being and the ability to promote chi absorption, store chi within, and balance chi not only assists body health but, perhaps surprisingly, mental and emotional health, too. As you learn T'ai Chi, your body is taught how to become vastly more energy efficient by the movements. The balance achieved physically is later achieved mentally and emotionally. Your night's rest will improve—sleep will come more easily and will stay longer as a result of your muscles being truly relaxed and ready to support your sleep as you climb into bed. Proper chi flow is a major contributor to deep and dreamless sleep. As your sleep improves, your anxiety will diminish.

Probably the biggest challenge you will face in learning T'ai Chi is getting the sequences committed to your mental memory and then to your muscle memory. It takes a while. But in the very nature of the effort is the aforementioned daily improvement of your physical nature. As you learn your sequences, even if it is a bit of a struggle, you will be gently stimulating your nervous system with new information, and your nervous system loves that! As a result of this moderate stimulation, your senses wake up. Colors will be brighter, food will be tastier, and the world becomes more alive and filled with variety. Your senses will open the pleasures of life to you, perhaps better than ever before.

As your senses expand, an equal opposite will also begin to occur. Your ability to focus when you want, and release your focus at will, will obviously increase. This is a wonderful freedom, to focus and problem solve as needed, and release the mental focus, along with the problem when you're done. This facilitating of one's focus is basic in the steps of learning. You will be bringing your body movements in line with your mental commands. It sounds plebeian, but in fact very little of our waking life is lived with body, mind, and emotions all doing one thing as a singular focus. To acquire this state is to be able to focus one's entire being on one goal—a process that is unifying, satisfying, and usually comforting. As you train your mind to guide your body, you will develop a communication between your body and mind. Eventually your practice will create a stable environment for this alliance to grow and at this point it will become clear how life itself also contributes to this awesome alliance.

Think about it. Your mind's desire is to search out information, solve dilemmas, meet life's challenges, and build a life well lived. However, your body's desire is security. These are two very different drives and, if undisciplined, can leave you always feeling the pull of both. For example: I'm hungry (body); no, don't eat, I'll get fat (mind). I'm sleepy (body); no, not yet (mind). I need a vacation (body); nope, not enough money (mind). I want to take that class (mind); nope, too tired (body). I need more rest to think (mind); nope, I'm craving ice cream (body). I need to figure out some new investments (mind); I'm terrified of losing my comforts (body). This list goes on. In each scenario they are not giving the needed support for success that is accomplished when both mind and body are on board, looking the same way. This requires a respectful awareness of the needs of both.

In ways that are not easy to analyze, T'ai Chi strengthens the alliance and lessens the tension. The most immediate benefit of this is a more youthful life view that is positive and enthusiastic. Very often a more youthful appearance will also result.

> Your mind—in the past, in the future. Your experience—in the present.

> Be still. Your mind quiets and steadies. Now you are ready For calm.

> Be calm. Be complete. Be free of desire for more.

Breath should
be smooth:
Calms mind and
provides better
energy movement.

Lift your head up—
string pulls upward
Your breath will
soften, smooth—
Now your mind
will still.

This tension between the security drives of the body and the creative drives of the mind account for far more stress, illness, and early aging that we often recognize.

Slowing down in our multi-layered world is becoming an art in and of itself, rushing from one thing to the next and feeling the pressure of time is an everyday reality. Sitting down, gathering oneself, a quiet moment of contemplation, a talk with a good friend—you may find that all of these become better when you move into the slow, underwater grace of T'ai Chi once a day. Match the movement with a quieting and deepening of breath, and you have left the unpleasant aspects of the day completely out of your practice. When you are finished with your practice, you will have a new lease on life and will be better able to make a decision about how much stress to accept back into your responses to life.

The quieting leads to an even more wonderful skill: resiliency. This word identifies the ability to return to elastic, flexible strength after being bent, compressed, or stretched. It holds within it the definition of how to snap back from illness, loss, depression, adversity, and so on and on and on. The ability to spring back, to rebound, may be one of life's greatest skills. T'ai Chi, without a doubt, facilitates this emotional and mental skill. By slowing down, opening the senses to the very present moment, deepening the breath, balancing the life-giving chi, and enjoying the sensuous pleasure of your practice, it serves as an islet of quiet. The more you can have life's challenges at the door of your practice space and just step into the form and focus on the movements, the more you will find resiliency available to you.

Improved resiliency helps depression. It's great to combine better breathing, and gentle movement to stimulate your endorphins and increase chi. If you are on medication, make a joint decision with your doctor about T'ai Chi's value and how best to reap the benefits for yourself.

The return of balance to your body-mind can surprise you with decreased cravings. As you become healthier, your unhealthy habits may become more manageable. Counseling and support can combine with T'ai Chi to help students and teachers alike have happier and healthier lives.

After the needed period of practice and incorporation into your life—six weeks to six months—you will notice a reduction of your general everyday vulnerability to stress. You will also find that a continued daily practice prevents stressful reactions before they start.

T'ai Chi over Fifty

There is a wonderful story about learning to improve life using the Eastern philosophical approach. A highly educated, well traveled Westerner arranged an appointment with a master teacher. By way of introducing himself, he told the teacher his name and just a few of his considerable accomplishments. The master smiled, offered him a seat, and invited him to tea. The Westerner gladly accepted. The master poured tea into his guest's cup until it was full, then overflowing, down the table, and onto the floor. Still he poured. Finally his guest could contain himself no longer. "The cup is full. You can't fit anymore into it!" "Yes," replied the master, "you are like the cup. Already so full there is no space for anything else. Learn about emptiness, then return to me."

Like the guest we have five, six, seven, or more decades under our belt. We are full of ideas, opinions, lifestyle habits, etc. But to really enjoy life as it is, to be in the present moment, to have the skills to adjust to the unexpected events of life, a bit of emptying must occur to create a place for the new to enter. The idea is appealing and makes sense as well, but the actual integration of this state of being is problematic. But not if you do T'ai Chi. Pursuing the motions and becoming familiar with the sequences and rhythms engages you in the act of becoming a bit empty. And that is a good thing, something from which many, many other good things evolve.

> T'ai Chi is infinity, the absolute: It creates from "no limit." It contains dynamic and static movement; it is the mother of yin and yang, of everything male and female. It is the root of motion, which is division, and of stillness, which is union. It must be neither overdone nor underdone . . . it must be exact.
> —Wang Chung-Yueh

It really makes no difference if you are a martial arts master or a retiree with some achy joints and a few free hours—the goal for a rich and satisfying life is the great leveler. The movements have endured for thousands of years because they contribute to and support a goal that bonds us all as one. T'ai Chi, through its simple, graceful, and flowing movements, presents us with an opportunity to promote vital longevity. And because the basic focus of T'ai Chi is to direct chi as a means to promoting a good, healthy life, there is a very high percentage of those practicing T'ai Chi are over fifty. In China, T'ai Chi has long been practiced well into the advancing years. T'ai Chi is cherished as a perfect vehicle to enable the years beyond fifty to indeed be filled with health, wisdom, joy of a life fully lived, and pleasure taken into each precious moment.

One very unique and endearing quality of T'ai Chi is that it is one of the only exercise activities that is timeless in its welcome. Most sports and physical activities become hazardous and even impossible as our bodies age. As time marches on, it is as if our bodies are developing a life of their own. Various aches and pains become apparent, recovery from illness can become tediously

> Be present.
> All will learn
> from your silence.

slow, and getting sick or injured seems to be, unfortunately, easier to accomplish. It is thrilling to experience a lessening of these challenges and the commensurate burdens associated with them. "This is how I felt twenty years ago," is a common comment from practitioners. To be able to bring the vitality and health of our youth through the self-awareness and wisdom of our maturity is the best of both worlds.

If you continue to deepen your release into the form during your daily practice, the gifts will also deepen. Body, mind, emotions, and your spiritual life will all be positively affected. A feeling of balance and comfort with one's unique niche in life is restored. Actually much of T'ai Chi is a restoration and enhancement process: restoring that which is our birthright in health, well-being, and self-acceptance; enhancing each part of us as we deepen our ability to be released into the gifts that are generated from the actions of T'ai Chi.

T'ai Chi is truly a come-as-you-are activity. Tall or short, young or old, sedentary or active, heavy or thin are all perfect in T'ai Chi's eyes. You don't have to become more limber, have more strength, more flexibility, stop smoking, reduce food intake, be young, and so on. However you are, wherever you are, whoever you are, T'ai Chi will receive you—right now—as is. Start, find your own experience, and progress at your own rate. T'ai Chi awaits you.

Part One

Understanding T'ai Chi

chapter 1

The History of T'ai Chi Ch'uan and T'ai Chi

The roots of T'ai Chi are hidden in the misty veil of secrecy that permeates many aspects of Chinese history. As a result, there are a variety of colorful stories about the roots of T'ai Chi. What is clear is that T'ai Chi as we know it has emerged from the martial art T'ai Chi Ch'uan. Before we look at the beginnings of this martial art, we must first understand the context in which it was developed.

Life in Ancient China

Ancient China was an extremely structured, rule-defined culture. At one point they had rules of behavior for every situation in all walks of life. There were even rules for how you exited the bathtub, sipped your tea, or greeted a friend. These rules also extended to rigid socio-economic class definition. The clothes worn, level of education, type of speech, lifestyle, and type of home all identified one's location in fulfilling a certain role in the culture. To present yourself as a teacher when you had been assigned by birth the role of a money lender was cause for punishment. Farmers gave birth to farmers, tailors to tailors, royals to royals. In our culture of personal independence and achievement, this type of culture can appear rigid and stifling. The political and philosophical reasoning behind this was two-fold: Politically it created great stability in a huge country. Philosophically it empowered each person to think of themselves as part of a great working culture—each person was responsible for completely embodying who they were in the culture and to then develop themselves to the fullest within that niche. In this way each person was a perfect part of a culture of wholeness. To learn and benefit from one's place in life, one's place in the order of it all, the niche had to be fully embodied, rather than resisted and changed. In this way, and in only this way, was the path to understanding the true meaning of life found. Certainly the systems engendered much seeming inequality, but what also occurred was the master attainment of becoming completely who you were and taking it, humble or grand, to an elevation of personal excellence.

Honesty, simplicity, and embracing one's part in the whole were woven into the very fabric of Chinese life. Becoming the best you could be, whatever your niche in life, through a personal exploration of art, music, philosophy, and martial arts, as well as an appreciation of nature's beauty and wisdom facilitated a striving for excellence rarely seen in other cultures. It was from these high standards that the martial arts masters emerged.

The feudal world of China was filled with internal and external conflict. Some men were born into a warrior family but the need for warriors became so great that many others were conscripted into service. By breaking the rigidly held cultural structure, a fresh pool of talent was allowed to develop new skills—from this talent came the great masters. This was one of the few areas of class structure where social status could be achieved not by birth, but by talent alone. The tools required for achieving status and success were found in the temples of training, and the martial arts were the key to great achievement. The competition for training was fierce. Many warriors became grist for the war mills, but some men of great talent and skill survived and went on to pursue an excellence in their art still not seen duplicated in our modern world.

> Adopt the pace of nature, patience.

> Many T'ai Chi teachers have gone before you. Learn and find your own T'ai Chi, not theirs.

The Chinese culture's devotion to personal excellence and reverence for natural beauty produced a most unique warrior-monk. Inner peace was embodied as a choice and guided by acceptance of one's role in life and one's place in the culture. Though exposed to the horror and chaos of war, it was counterbalanced with the learned attunement to the serenity of nature—a discipline that allowed the men to be in inner quiet as they went about the grisly business of war.

The Development of T'ai Chi Ch'uan

As warriors trained in martial skills, what we now know as T'ai Chi Ch'uan began to emerge. T'ai Chi Ch'uan provided a format to join these dual, seemingly opposite, skills of inner and outer strength. This satisfied two high priorities: to be a great warrior and yet to be filled with inner peace and quiet. The men who could be completely calm and controlled in battle were the best warriors. The inner grace and attunement to chi required to maintain this unusual state of awareness was slowly accumulated as T'ai Chi Ch'uan strength and agility training progressed.

During this time T'ai Chi Ch'uan became the cornerstone of the martial arts temple schools that dotted China's landscape. These temple schools sought to produce men who expressed supreme physical and spiritual development. The

In the 1800s a very old manuscript was found in a salt shop, of all places. The man who found it took it to his brother, Wu Yu-hsiang (1812–1880). His brother was a T'ai Chi Ch'uan student of the Chen family. Wu then showed the interesting manuscript to his honored teacher, Yang Lu-shan (1800–1873). To the delight and astonishment of them both, they were able to confirm the manuscript was from the great Wu Tang monk—Zhang San Feng.

graduate monk-warriors became the revered moral backbone of the ancient Chinese culture, and since they were expected to get better as they got older, they developed tools to support that quest. T'ai Chi Ch'uan became one of the best ways to fulfill their goal—it became the supportive structure for the pursuit of and accomplishment in martial arts, spiritual training, artistic training, and radiant health and longevity. As a result, the knowledge of how to practice T'ai Chi and reap the benefit of longevity became a treasure more valuable than gold—and it was knowledge as guarded as a hidden treasure, passed on in a concealed tradition, carefully protected from outsiders.

The Founders of T'ai Chi Ch'uan

The history of T'ai Chi Ch'uan is entertaining and a bit varied and credits many different individuals for its development. The earliest recorded reference to T'ai Chi Ch'uan (A.D. 600–900) is from a Chinese hermit, Xu Xuan Ping. He practiced and passed along an art known as the Thirty-Seven Patterns of T'ai Chi Ch'uan. This first form of T'ai Chi Ch'uan was called *Changquan*, Long Fist. Always looking to nature's inspiration, it was named with the Yangtze River in mind because these movements were to be as long and continuous as that great river.

As often happens, another man, a Taoist priest from the Wudang Mountain Temple named Li Dao Zi, was developing another, similar sequence of movements at the same time (A.D. 618–906). It is generally believed these two concurrent teachers provided the foundation for T'ai Chi as we know it today.

The first time T'ai Chi Ch'uan was found in a classical text was Chen Ling Xi's *The Method to Attain Enlightenment through Observing the Scripture*, in the Tang Dynasty (907–973). Having achieved the balance of the outer warrior and inner monk, Chen Ling Xi promoted a new long-term goal: to attain balance and become an enlightened, perfect man. This accomplishment required years of training in T'ai Chi Ch'uan, and so the perfect examples were always older adults, honored and revered by all.

Zhang San Feng

Zhang San Feng (also spelled Chang San-feng) is sometimes credited with being the person who provided the conduit through which T'ai Chi Ch'uan merged the inner quest of monks with the martial arts. Zhang San Feng was a graduate of the Shoalin Monastery and a master teacher in the warrior tradition. He lived toward the end of the Song Dynasty (A.D. 1200) and in the time of the Yuan Dynasty, known chiefly for the leadership of the Mongol Kubla Khan, and their frequent visitor, Marco Polo.

Zhang San Feng had studied Kung Fu, Qigong movement, and Zen, and then left the Shoalin Monastery to continue his studies at the Purple Summit Temple, the most sacred temple for the pursuit of Taoism, a philosophy of life that was taught by Lao Tzu, the great Chinese philosopher, and embraced by virtually all monk-warriors.

The development of T'ai Chi Ch'uan took a dramatic turn when Zhang San Feng had an epiphany about the importance of combining power with grace in which he realized that he witnessed these movements in nature. He observed a fight between a snake and a bird. Some say a sparrow, others say a crane. It was a fight to the death. As the bird struck, the snake would gracefully avoid the striking bill. With a serpentine movement of deadly grace, the snake bought time. Swaying gracefully, appearing vulnerable, the snake slowly brought the bird into its control and then, when it was fully in charge and ready, it struck and won the battle.

Watching the graceful and yet very forceful combat, Zhang San Feng became a man inspired. He took his new-found understanding of the importance of controlling another through calm, purposeful, controlled grace and blended it with the existing martial arts. He accomplished this by modifying the outwardly forceful, coarse movements of Shaolin Kung Fu. The T'ai Chi Ch'uan that he developed included breath work, channeling chi, inner visualizations, and an emphasis on sensing the intent as well as seeing the action of one's opponent. This has evolved to be the T'ai Chi Ch'uan we know today.

Li Dao Zi's Thirty-Seven Movements had given Zhang San Feng the practical tool to fulfill his vision of a new and better martial art. And it did indeed accomplish his desire. Both of the goals of enhanced fighting skill and undisturbed inner quiet were blended, and unexpectedly there also emerged a state of much greater health and well-being.

> T'ai Chi Ch'uan was for many years used only for self-defense and combat. There were three clearly defined components to the art: The postures, push-hands, and handling weapons. The postures were at first much more strenuous. It is these postures that have evolved into the Yang style of T'ai Chi.

Today T'ai Chi practitioners reap the benefits of health, well-being, and inner calm. Zhang San Feng is cherished by many T'ai Chi practitioners as the revered patriarch of T'ai Chi Ch'uan. From him comes the understanding of how to develop one's inner chi to facilitate outer resilience. He is often seen as the man who started the long lineage of masters who have created the Supreme Ultimate in health and well-being, a wellspring of internal vitality and strength.

The work of Zhang San Feng divided eventually into the three trunks of the T'ai Chi Ch'uan: Pakua Kungfu, Hsing yi Kungfu, and T'ai Chi Ch'uan.

> T'ai Chi Ch'uan's wise elder Zhang San Feng's great wish for T'ai Chi Ch'uan was not teaching martial art techniques alone, but to promote the attainment of vital longevity for everyone.

The Spread of T'ai Chi Ch'uan

T'ai Chi Ch'uan was taught in a one to one relationship. It was transmitted from a skilled master to a carefully chosen student and never taught in large classes. The relationship between them excluded all others. The student essentially surrendered every other aspect of his life to train with his master. It was a very demanding and cherished relationship in which the master became a mentor, sharing all he knew for the betterment and continued excellence of T'ai Chi Ch'uan.

In the classic master-student tradition, Zhang San Feng transmitted in temple seclusion his T'ai Chi Ch'uan knowledge to his chosen student, Tai yi Zhenrin. Tai yi Zhenrin was a Taoist priest valued long into his later years as a magnificent swordsman in the Wudang tradition. He then continued the concealed master/mentor-student relationship by teaching his student of choice, and the lineage continued.

By the end of the Ming Dynasty (1368–1644) T'ai Chi Ch'uan, responding to the unification of all China, slowly seeped beyond the martial art temples and into Taoist temples and other, secular disciplines throughout the country. This was not a smooth transition, because the T'ai Chi Ch'uan secret movements had become essential for maintaining a power base in an unsettled world. But slowly they seeped out through a cautious transmission, and always to men, never to women.

Development of the Yang Form

The Yang form of T'ai Chi, the form you will be learning in *Stay Young with T'ai Chi*, has its own history. The original messenger of Yang style T'ai Chi, Yang Lew Shan (also spelled Yang Lew Chen), was born to farmers in a province of China known as Ho-Pei. Being born from a lineage of feast-or-famine farmers in 1799, he had a body honed remarkably well for martial arts. Slender, lithe, efficient, and small, he had self-discipline in his genes and an efficient use of food and energy in his bones.

He became interested in the martial arts, and his interest led him to seek instruction. An elderly boxer, Shao-Lin, trained him initially in a style of hard boxing that was made up of thirty-three long-form movements. It was through the encouragement of this initial teacher that he heard of the Chen family.

The Chen family was a secretive, jealous guardian of T'ai Chi Ch'uan and unwilling to train anyone who was not a Chen. Yang was refused as a student. Undeterred, he sought work on the Chen family farm and over time he made his way into acceptance. The stories vary but what is clear is that somehow he impressed the Chens enough, was accepted as a student and allowed entrance into their private and guarded compound.

Not being a valued student or a high-ranking son, Yang was most likely overlooked for quite a while. He found he could sneak a peek at the practices done by the Chens and not be noticed, and in private he put the practices he witnessed to fruitful use. As his skill increased, he eventually came to be noticed by the Chens as a force to reckon with. He was matched against many of their kind, his skill allowing him to win consistently. As his skills continued to increase, the Chen family shared more and more of their secrets with him. This was to our own great advantage because at this point Yang, now magnificently trained, return to his home in the Ho-Pei province and began to teach T'ai Chi Ch'uan to his interested friends and neighbors. The binding ties of secrecy were finally broken and T'ai Chi Ch'uan began to seep into the world beyond its sequestered roots.

Of course, its great value was perceived at once—and it was exciting for people to be learning an art spoken of and rumored about for two thousand years, but never before shared. Yang taught many and became well known for his approach to T'ai Chi Ch'uan, which became known as Yang's T'ai Chi. So impressive were his skills at both demonstrating and teaching Yang T'ai Chi that he was even invited to the enclosed palace to teach the royal family.

One of the most stunning testimonies to Yang's skill was that although he fought full-on, matching skills over and over again, he was so skilled that in his matches he never seriously hurt any of the men. This demonstrated a level of skill that defined a great goal. It was through this consistent skill that he won the hearts and minds of many, many Chinese people. Throughout his years of travel and contest, he never lost, he never seriously hurt an opponent, and due to his sense of fair play and honor, he made no enemies. The people often called him by another name: Yang Wu-Ti, which means Yang No Enemy or No Rival.

His strength and its source remained a mystery to everyone who witnessed it. The martial arts and the magical relationship to strength that disciplined chi will allow had never been seen beyond the temple and compound walls. As a small, wiry man, Yang appeared to have no real strength in his muscles when he moved. He was light, not dense. He was lithe, not powerful and solid. He moved gracefully, like a dancer, not clumping along, muscle-bound with a heavy torso. He looked so lightweight that when reality showed itself, he could toss men twice his size into the air, as if they were sticks, and it looked like a wonderful magic. Since no one understood through their own experience the source of his strength, many stories,

Ancient China is known for its excellence in many areas. These are generally seen as poetry, calligraphy, music, painting, Taoist philosophy, and T'ai Chi Ch'uan. The Chinese sought to develop each one of these skills as their years progressed so as to be a balanced and "supreme" man by the end of their years.

legends, and fables grew around him as he traveled and taught. His ability to toss an adversary back as if he weighed as much as a feather was breathtaking. He mastered the spear and became skilled in making his chi "sticky." Combining these skills, he could lift objects that weren't too heavy on the tip of his spear with great grace. He needed no conventional bow for his arrows. He simply used the lightning speed of his arm and fingers to propel the arrow to the target. He hit the target with consistent success. Wherever he went, he achieved status as a master. Feted, fed, enjoyed, and now famous, he was welcomed into the homes and hearts of many, many Chinese.

Continuing Yang's Tradition

Yang married and his wife gave him three sons. Much to their sorrow, their firstborn died in childhood. The other two went on to become T'ai Chi masters in their own right. The second son, Yang-Yu, took over much of the instruction and provided some relief for his father by catering to the constant demands of potential students. Yang-Yu never really received the recognition for this he deserved. People so wanted to be taught by Yang Lew Shan that, even though instructed by his son, they credited their training to his father and claimed Yang Lew Shan as their personal teacher.

> The final goal of T'ai Chi is to embody the state of internal illumination, which is called the Pearls of Elixir.

Yang-Yu was an ardent student of his father's, constantly honing and expanding his skill despite the extremes in weather. In the martial arts, discipline was mandatory and if the student seemed to be lagging, punishment was the order of the day, and so it was with Yang Lew Shan. He laid a whip to his son's back many times to impress a point upon him. The harsh and unforgiving training from his father drove Yang-Yu very close to abandoning home and father to gain relief. He did stay, though, and he emulated his father's strong personality. He frequently sought challenges and managed easily to thrust his opponents back eight to ten feet. Despite his successes, his father found ways for him to correct his form. Yang-Yu continued his ascent toward mastery of T'ai Chi Ch'uan, but dropped back from teaching. Instead he invested himself in developing great inner force. One of his favorite personal demonstrations was to put a few grains of rice on his very well trained abdomen. By saying "Haah!" and projecting his chi, he could toss them to the ceiling.

The third son, Yang-Chian, was also deeply troubled by his father's harsh discipline and lack of tenderness. He sought relief from the rigorous home environment that was filled with discipline. He was ready to shave his long braid and become a Buddhist monk, but his family dissuaded him.

It is clear from these stories how difficult and demanding Yang was as a teacher. Few students stayed with him for long periods of time, for it would push them beyond what they could endure. Yang's sons, however, brought a good nature to the work and the value of T'ai Chi spread and deepened. The introduction of a more human approach to the learning was essential to the Yang T'ai Chi story. Had the finest training also stayed so harsh, very few would have learned it well. With the gentler sons, the training continued in excellence and became more accessible to a greater number of people. In this way, T'ai Chi Ch'uan made its way to the people. Yang Lew Shan was the bridge and his sons became the first part of the path many ordinary people now move along.

The skills Yang-Chian developed and then excelled at were somewhat different from those of his father. He, like his father, was good with spears and also sticks. He could apply what appeared to be minimum strength to them and still his opponents were knocked to the ground. He had an amazing skill with his chi. He could hold a bird in his palm and would slowly draw his palm downward, as he did this, the bird would be unable to free itself to fly away. His awareness was such that, like the masters mentioned in the wonderful book *Graceful Exits*, he knew a few hours before his death that his time was arriving. Old and ready, he gathered friends and family and had the time to bid them goodbye. He then took a bath, dressed in fresh clothes, and passed from his body.

His heirs were his two sons. The first and third lived to adulthood. The middle one died in childhood. The eldest son bore traits very similar to his famous and revered grandfather. He was aggressive and liked to attack his opponent. He also shared the capacity for physical abuse when his student didn't measure up. Again T'ai Chi Ch'uan stumbled in its expansion because so few students stayed with Chao-Hsiung. He was, nonetheless, skilled in wonderful ways. His ability with chi showed itself when he would amaze others by moving a candle with his mind with such speed the flame would be put out. This ability has been lost, for now, in the T'ai Chi teachings, but as we all become proficient with chi, it could return.

The third son of Yang-Chian, Chao-Chin, was an enigma in the family and lived out his father's peaceful nature. He was not drawn to T'ai Chi Ch'uan and had an interesting personal philosophy: "It is not worth learning to be one man's enemy. It is worth learning to be the enemy of a thousand men." But with his grandfather's insistence that he learn T'ai Chi Ch'uan, he began to have an altogether different vision of the martial art. He understood clearly that it would improve the health and physical condition of the entire nation if it was taught with this goal in mind. After his father died he came very much into his own. He developed the "iron fist in the soft glove" approach and worked with remarkable diligence and exhibited a great talent, especially since he was mostly self-taught.

The current form of Yang T'ai Chi is comfortable, stable, light, and pleasurable. It is this style that we owe to Chao-Chin, who was also known as Chen-Fu.

This journey of T'ai Chi Ch'uan's evolution started in 1799 with the birth of the tough and disciplined disciplinarian Yang Lew Shan and continues in this moment in time. As T'ai Chi Ch'uan has spread, it has indeed stepped back from the harsh abuse that was so much a part of its lineage of training warriors. The softness and grace that now mark T'ai Chi is a useful adaptation. Once again, T'ai Chi has shown its enormous value by being a flexible form of movement so deeply rooted in the garnering and dispersal of chi that the change still produces wonderful enhancement in vitality and longevity for its students. The world is changing now, and it is more important to become proficient in sensitive word use and intuitive chi sensitivity within the form of dialogue and conversation. The way of the warrior is slowly giving way to brotherhood. T'ai Chi supports this transition with its own undiminished effectiveness in contributing so generously to the well-being of humankind. Becoming familiar with chi and the marvelous recognitions and awareness that chi engenders facilitates this all important transition that humankind is now making. In understanding the evolution of T'ai Chi, it becomes clear that it has consistently dovetailed with the evolution of humankind.

When you step into learning the basic flow of T'ai Chi, acknowledge and assume a stance of gratitude for the variety of people who have passed this on to you, for the devotion, abusive or gentle, that they gave to this, and for the great, fervent hope they passed along with it that it would be carried well guarded as a precious gem and then given the time to develop and expand so its gifts would be there for anyone who does T'ai Chi.

As with all ancient arts, the more you do it, the easier it gets and the more it demonstrates its humbling effectiveness. T'ai Chi remains a much studied form of martial art. It is now sought primarily for its health and well-being benefits, but still inherent in the movement is the potential for spiritual growth—not a religious belief, but a spiritual attunement that supports and enriches any faith and religion. In all dimensions of our being T'ai Chi provides a rich venue for life enhancement.

Chapter 2

Chi

C hi is the Chinese word for the core vital life energy that emanates from and brings continued vitality to all of life. Chi permeates all living things and empowers, enlivens, and animates movement—from the moving molecules of rocks and the agitation of a tornado to human vitality, chi animates all. Chi is the essence of vitality and it fills us according to our capacity to absorb it, nurture it, and garnish it. All things are filled with chi and all of life is bound together by the flow of chi.

Chi is the very center of the Chinese and T'ai Chi approach to health and well-being. Just as a spring bubbling to earth's surface brings life to all that surrounds it, so chi brings life to all that it flows through. The area surrounding the spring will thrive in direct relationship to the amount of water it can receive. Routing the water through the deliberate intent of damming rivers takes the precious water into specific areas to ensure that area's flourishing. A wise and clear person will watch the spring and study its affect on the surrounding area carefully. With gentle persuasion based on educated observation, this wise person will encourage water to distribute in a way that the entire area grows more beautifully. Some things will need less water, others more, and others will have inherent weaknesses that require a specific flow be designed just for them. This is a well-used metaphor for describing the proper relationship each person can have to their personal spring of life, their chi flow, wisely tending the health and well-being of mind, spirit, and body.

The ancient Chinese who came to recognize chi's ever present power, became intent on having complete knowledge of chi. What is it? Where does it come from? What does its existence mean? What is it here to teach? The questions then refined to the next level as the recognition of the properties and meaning of chi evolved: How can it be cultivated? How can it be refined? How can it serve humanity's ability to reach its full potential for life and liveliness?

To be supple is Qi, to be hard and strong is to block Qi.

Are there any limits in chi? How can we know as much as possible about this precious source of life and liveliness? As these questions formed and recognition was pursued, many influences of chi started to become apparent. Because chi is life, nothing is able to live without it; to truly live to limitless potential, chi had to be understood absolutely.

Over time many insights into chi emerged: Chi is a current of liveliness that animates and brings life to *everything*. Chi travels in tandem with air. Within this current of life high and low vibrations are present simultaneously. High is good. Low is not so good. Low vibration chi encourages difficult emotions such as rage, possessiveness, and greed. Low vibrating chi reduces and even destroys the spiritual potential of lives. High vibration chi, on the other hand, facilitates the ability to have clear perspective on life and to know one's place within life and to be filled with the peace that passes all understanding.

In the same way, low or poorly balanced chi brings low energy and fragile health (definitely undesirable on the martial arts battle front), while a high level of well-balanced chi aids high, consistent energy and buoyant, durable health, as well as speedy recovery from wounds and illness.

When the chi is full and nurtured it facilitates animation and when the chi is low there is a commensurate reduction in aliveness and animation. A person filled with chi will be as bright eyed, supple, and eager for life as a child. Even if they are clearly older, the aliveness is full to brimming. A person low on chi, no matter what age, will be the opposite—low energy, dull in curiosity, with generally reduced liveliness, even listless. The expectation is that this state of slow reduction of aliveness is the natural state of aging. But this it not so—it is the natural outcome of the unnatural state of reduced chi.

T'ai Chi and Qigong are two of the most effective ways to come into initial awareness of chi—and the bounty of well-being their harvest bequeaths.

Cultivating Chi through T'ai Chi

As T'ai Chi is practiced, a variety of things occur. Breath is taken in deeply. Chi is extracted from the air and intentionally directed into the important internal energy center called the *tan t'ien*, in which the chi is stored, increased, and garnered. The tan t'ien is an internal place buried deep within the pelvis, about one and a half inches below the navel back in the center of the pelvis. The chi is directed from the tan t'ien to then circulate throughout the body on meridians. The meridians, energy highways that travel through the body, disperse the chi from the tippy top of the head down to the toes, throughout all the organs, brain and skin, everywhere, and generally keeps the body healthy and full of life and in balance.

In order to create a chi-receptive body, you need movement coupled and coordinated with breath. Movement creates body alertness and chi brings an infusion of the required vital spark. Because chi is constantly being gathered, accumulated, and dispersed, it becomes critical to have an activity that brings a constant, steady state of movement to the pelvis and that the movement be effectively coordinated with the chi-filled breath. Furthermore, since chi is stored in the tan t'ien, it becomes essential to bring correct chi-enhancing movement to the hips. These movements support the chi in radiating throughout the entire body from the tan t'ien, pelvis, and hips.

> We know natural breathing as children, before life's stresses build up within.

The larger chi picture is something like this: We are living in a vital web of universally created chi. We gain access to chi by absorbing it. The internalized chi is our life energy. As chi disperses throughout the body, it balances and refines according to the nature of earth. Chi first divides into two separate but interdependent flows—yin, the feminine receptive flow, and yang, the masculine assertive flow. These flows travel throughout the body on chi veins, or meridians. The yin and yang flows further refine into the five basic elements of the earth: earth, wood, fire, metal, and water. Upon exhalation, the chi returns to the universal chi field to unite once again with eternity, the great void—*Wu Chi*.

The movements of T'ai Chi are intricately crafted to engage the source of chi (Wu Chi), direct its earthly dispersal, and return the chi to the great void. It is through the attention to this interaction that T'ai Chi brings you its great gifts.

All of T'ai Chi is formed to contain and direct. This is accomplished through precise movement, relaxation into the movement or form, and breath control. The vital force increases, as it finds freedom to flow through receptive muscles and organs, health issues improve and sometimes even go away.

As the precise T'ai Chi movements are performed, they are not difficult. One such movement in which chi permeates muscles, tissues, joints, organs, and bones more effectively is the thirty percent/seventy percent stance. This engages the concept of adjusting the inner feeling, or chi weight, of one leg to feeling almost empty, seventy percent empty (or seventy percent yin), and thirty percent full (or thirty percent yang). While you direct the other leg to feel almost full, seventy percent full, or yang, and thirty percent empty or yin. This is the thirty percent-seventy percent stance, and you can become familiar with it as you sit and read this. Put more weight on one foot and lighten up on the other. As your muscles tense to direct weight to your foot, that leg becomes seventy percent full. Simultaneously, let the other leg relaxes, or empties. That is thirty percent empty. Your best attempt is perfect. Now, shift the weight of the feet and shift the seventy percent-thirty percent in the legs. Seventy percent is heavier, thirty percent lighter. You have directed the chi with mind and movement. Don't make it hard. It isn't. You are on your way.

As you practice Qigong or T'ai Chi, there will be a great and perhaps new-for-you focus on your tan t'ien—the potent, centering power source within. You will be learning a variety of breathing exercises to focus and enhance your abilities with chi. This is called *Tao Yie* (pronounced DAO YEE). Tao means outer development. Yie means internal development. To do Tao Yie is to develop your internal chi field and strengthen your relationship to the external chi field.

To achieve Tao Yie, you will learn to *To Noa* (pronounced DU NOW), the actual breath exercises. To is to exhale carbon dioxide and low-energy chi, and Noa is to inhale fresh gases and fresh chi. To do To Noa implies the learning and eventual mastery of two aspects of chi cultivation. The first is the internalizing of ever-increasing amounts of chi. The second is the all-important methods for encouraging the chi to penetrate every part of the entire body. Breathing is an important half (but only half) of the complete picture. In order to have optimum health, you learn how to direct your chi to various areas. Directing chi and incorporating it into the body is the essential other half. Areas vulnerable to illness and injury are, for whatever reason, more resistant to balanced fresh chi, but also need chi to become healthy again. Persistent Tao Yie will solve the problem and assist this ascent of vitality.

There will be a sample of breath chi exercises later in the book for you to try. The precise skills of To Noa are best learned in the traditional, tried and true way: directly from a teacher of your choice.

Toning your chi on a daily basis creates great vitality and inner peace. This daily commitment also connects the internal chi field—the flow of chi in your body—to the external chi field that simultaneously connect us to all of life, on earth and beyond. It is this merging, when the sense of personal boundaries fade for a moment, that occurs when the T'ai Chi practitioner has a personal experience of oneness with a surrounding environment. At that moment one is filled with an understanding of love and harmony. It is through this inner alignment and the outer increased sensitivity to oneness that true inner peace is achieved. It is to this end that all the uniquely patterned T'ai Chi movements, the body alignment, and the breath awareness are moving. Each day is different and filled with new challenges, new gifts and, always, great potential. So you must align yourself to the various subtle changes in chi on a daily basis. In doing this, the subtle alignments in the relationship between the outer chi field and your inner chi field are corrected. As a result, your body joins the day. It will know how to take in, disperse, and balance chi beautifully. It is this simple concept that

Chi will fill your body. This enhances a greater feeling of well-being. This feeling of internal well-being is essential for a good, resilient approach to life. As our bodies start down the path of having a life of their own separate from our will, a good, solid feeling of inner well-being is a golden gift. Once established, T'ai Chi and breath control will bring it returning again and again as life progresses. Since the experience of life unfolds in a mysterious and unpredictable way, it is very nice indeed to have this as a resource, right at your fingertips, so to speak. This tends to generate the faith that everything is progressing as it should and all is in its right place.

empowers the body to levels of health restoration and a wellspring of longevity that defies current scientific analysis.

Chi is a key to a deeper personal understanding of life as it is. It is personal, not something that can easily be shared and quantified. Like life, it is also a mystery. As a deeply personal experience it can be described to another, but the true experience is distinctly personal and as such stimulates unique personal growth or individuation. The great dichotomy of chi is that it joins all of life and translates the truth of all of life, but it is deeply and intensely personal in its interaction and method of communication. Gentle, wise, and all-knowing, chi is the voice of life and love. For this reason it has, and continues to capture the attention of thousands of people.

Chapter 3

T'ai Chi in Chinese Medicine

The source of all chi, liveliness, energy, and potential is called Wu Chi, which is the Chinese term for "great void." Wu Chi is the potential. This potential is activated when we practice T'ai Chi. Wu Chi is the emptiness prior to our T'ai Chi practice that we direct with our intention into our ability to live a healthy life. When we practice T'ai Chi our movements draw from this great void of unrealized potential, activate that potential with our intent, and impact our life as a result of the action. It is from Wu Chi that everything emerges. Wu Chi provides what is required for that spark of life to occur. Your idea, that moment when potential is drawn into the spark of life, is T'ai Chi. Your choice about how to direct the spark into action in and on life is affected by how you draw the contents of the chi—which comes from the Wu Chi, through the T'ai Chi, into you.

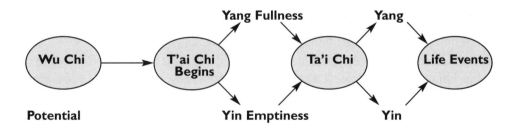

The Philosophy of Yin and Yang

The two forces of energy as expressed through Chinese philosophy are yin and yang. The chi that we are cultivating through T'ai Chi practice is ceaselessly made up of these two forces, which are the dualistic components of all life.

As you become more aware of the energetic connection of all things, you may become interested in learning more. There are many, many books written on this. Books on acupuncture, energy balancing of the meridians, energy massage, energetic meditations and inner visualizations, yoga, and many others. You might give Chinese herbs a try under the guiding hand of a well trained Chinese doctor or doctor of acupuncture. You might use a chart to see if a specific color can affect an emotional, mental, physical, or spiritual state. There are wonderful books, fascinating and thorough, awaiting you.

These two forces govern our bodies, our lives, nature, national and international events, and events throughout the universe.

The famous yin-yang sign is the visual symbol for the constantly coexisting yin and yang forces. The dark side represents yin and the small dot of white represents the bit of yang that is always present in yin. The light area represents yang and the small dot of black represents the bit of yin that is always present in yang. These two forces are completely interactive and their interaction is as eternal as the universe and as ceaseless as life. Although opposed to one another, they cannot be divided. Yin and yang co-exist in a circular or round relationship, just as depicted in the icon. This roundness is a counterclockwise energetic force that is as natural to life as cause and effect—both are forces of life, both by their nature co-exist. One cannot be without the other. Without cause, there would be no effect. Without effect, there would be no cause. Without yin, there could be no yang. Without yang, there could be no yin. We cannot conceive of life without these co-existing forces, for they are life.

In the Chinese system of health, the entire body is viewed in terms of yin and yang. Someone has a cold—to much yin. Someone else has a high fever—too much yang. The health of organs, bones, skin, hair—everything is integrated into this system. Each person interacts with this balance of yin and yang based on their own uniqueness. A genetically quiet (yin) person will automatically draw in more yin energy, while an aggressive (yang) person will automatically draw in more yang energy. Balancing yin and yang within the body is the essential component of great health and satisfying longevity.

How do yin and yang get out of balance? To the degree that the life we live is not in balanced accord with nature, we risk yin-yang imbalance. In the past hundred years our lives have changed enormously, and very few of the changes have been inspired by the desire to live in harmony with nature and universal wisdom. All of us are continually at risk of imbalance, but this doesn't necessarily mean our life will be shortened. What it does mean is that the quality of our personal life is compromised by the symptoms created by a lack of harmony. Anxiety, depression, loneliness, longing, regret, and fear are only a few of the symptoms of yin-yang imbalance.

Harmonizing Yin and Yang

T'ai Chi movements can increase accessibility through lengthening the moment that you are drawing in chi and simultaneously increase effective balancing of yin-yang energy. Over time, T'ai Chi movement corrects much of the imbalance between the energies. While practicing T'ai Chi it is important to embrace the knowledge of chi.

Our T'ai Chi intent merges with our T'ai Chi movement as one in the same moment. The liveliness of your intent, which draws from the pure emptiness of Wu Chi, divides the chi into yin and yang according to your nature. Angry— more yang. Sad—more yin. These two forces, shaped by original intent, then flow into our T'ai Chi movement. From this action springs our unique interaction with life.

The most common way to add intention to your practice is by praying, worshipping, or meditating. This can be done in an active state of walking or through practicing T'ai Chi or in a quiet state of sitting, kneeling, or standing. You will find that by asking for help with a humble heart before your T'ai Chi practice, your intention will alter your internal state of need. Another internal state will have been imparted that carries within it a fresh belief, more confidence, and better problem solving.

In addition to your intent, the movements will change the energies in you to be a balance of soft/grace and hard/force. If you start your T'ai Chi practice in harmony with the energies you are cultivating, it will help you to develop a soft, yin, approach to the form. As you continue your practice while nurturing the receptive yin to the extreme from this root of gentleness, then overtime the yang or the hard/force will begin to emerge into the form.

Think of metal. It is melted down to be made pliable and moldable. This is the metal's yin form. The metal's impurities are separated from it at this stage. When the metal has been purified so it is strong, not brittle—this is often done by pounding the metal—then it is ready to be formed as it hardens, the softness now co-existing as a seed within.

This analogy is a good one for understanding the introduction of T'ai Chi into the body. First the movements are done in flexible grace. In this open yielding the poor habits and structural difficulties become apparent. The student "pounds" these areas by first gently, and eventually more firmly, nudging them into relaxation, realignment, and release. As the form becomes more familiar, the structured influences within the form can now easily find their place. With each passing practice the form takes on more and more form, until the full structure of the form is embodied. When the full structure is embodied, the natural flow back to yin again occurs. Now softness co-exists with the form. Subtly moving with the form to create a far more refined comprehension of how softness influences,

> Because the Tao is not a faith—it is a philosophy of wholeness—it supports every personal faith.

and how hardness provides the fertile soil for softness. Rather than have one replace the other, they instead work together, flowing yang to yin and yin to yang, bringing the T'ai Chi practitioner ever more subtle experiences of these forces of life. It is through these embodied understandings that great life insights, personal revelations, and golden nuggets of wisdom emerge.

An absolute requirement for a satisfying life is to continually seek harmony and balance between these forces internally and externally. The Chinese process of properly combining these dual forces is called *tong-chin*. When one has achieved tong-chin, then the more magical aspects of inner and outer life become apparent, and the supernatural realms appear. Most of us are really not interested in these more advanced gifts attributed to tong-chin. It is enough for most to know that gaining knowledge of these forces is a wise choice.

To balance yin-yang is the very heart of our T'ai Chi. By bringing body-mind-breath into T'ai Chi, you teach your body to unite in harmony with these essential flows of life. This, in turn, affects and improves moods, thoughts, spiritual development, and body health. This entire process is learned through doing. It is your joyous responsibility to tend to your space with wisdom, tenderness, and self-love. T'ai Chi is the messenger that brings you the understanding of how to successfully tend your gift of life.

The Five Elements

According to Chinese medicine, yin and yang energies directly effect what are referred to as the five elements, which are the essential components that make up life. As yin and yang move within the body, they refine into these five elements: water, fire, wood, metal, and earth. Because we see these elements in nature, they may seem separate from us. However, they are considered to be an all-inclusive dynamic process that is basic to comprehending the movements of all life, including us. Each element carries its own unique properties, as shown in the following chart:

THE ESSENTIAL QUALITIES OF THE FIVE ELEMENTS

Element	Element Characteristic	Human Characteristic
Water	Soaks Descends	Receptive Deep
Fire	Heats Moves upward	Active Forward moving
Wood	Formed Can be reformed	Structured Interactive
Metal	Melting Molded Hardened	Transformative Creator of new Endurance
Earth	Provides nourishment Sowing and reaping	Maternal Creative Thriving

As the five elements course their way through our bodies, they make contact and are affected by one another. These interactions are predictable and are defined by four major principles: mutual creation, mutual closeness, mutual destruction, and mutual fear. These dynamic, life-giving interactions are outlined as follows.

Mutual Creation
One element produces the other in an endless cycle of creation:

Wood creates fire: By rubbing two sticks together fire occurs.

Fire creates earth: As fire burns ash is created and the ash becomes earth.

Earth creates metal: Metal is found within and has been made within earth.

Metal creates water: Dew forms on metal left out at night (this dew water was often used in healing), and metal melts into liquid.

Water creates wood: Water nourishes the plants and trees that wood forms.

This is a cycle of creation. You can enter the cycle at any point.

Mutual Closeness
This is seen as a relationship not unlike a mother and child, a natural, organic closeness of the element to its creator.

Wood is close to water.

Water is close to metal.

Metal is close to earth.

Earth is close to fire.

Fire is close to wood.

Mutual Destruction

This principle presents the conflicts that erupt between elements:

Wood weakens earth: It leaches its elements from it.

Earth limits water: It contains its movement, as in lakes and dams.

Water extinguishes fire.

Fire conquers metal: It weakens its great strength through melting it.

Metal destroys wood: It chops it down.

Mutual Fear

This means that an element has a respect for or a fear of the element that has the ability to destroy it.

Wood fears metal: Metal cuts wood.

Metal fears fire: Fire melts metal.

Fire fears water: Water extinguishes fire.

Water fears earth: Earth contains water.

Earth fears wood: Wood weakens earth's nourishment.

The Five Elements in Health and Well-Being

It is the composition or interaction of these elements within us that make up our nature person, give us clues to understanding and knowing ourselves and others better, and also give us vital information about the best route to health.

The elements and how they affect us is complex. A very simple tip of the iceberg follows:

Wood...... An active, direct person
Metal...... A contained person
Fire......... An intense, quick to respond person
Water...... An emotional person
Earth....... A solid, nurturing person

The five elements can also help us to diagnose or understand imbalances in our body that contribute to disease. The organs of the body are divided into: yin—solid organs; yang—hollow organs. Each organ has a corresponding element:

Heart ...... Fire   Small intestine .... Fire
Spleen ..... Earth   Stomach .... Earth
Lungs...... Metal   Large intestine....... Metal
Kidney .... Water   Bladder................. Water
Liver .... Wood   Gall Bladder .... Wood

This marvelous and simple theory of the five elements and their ever-changing relationship to one another throughout all of life—people and events—has been used with great wisdom in Chinese medicine. The goal is the maintenance of health and, if necessary, curing illness.

You can see in the following chart that everything is interrelated: chi, yin and yang, the five elements, our organs, and so on. These five elements create an interaction of wholeness—the aspects of nature, seasons, colors, and flavors are sustaining forces of our body.

Five Elements	Wood	Fire	Earth	Metal	Water
Directions	East	South	Center	West	North
Seasons	Spring	Summer	Long	Fall Summer	Winter
Colors	Blue	Red	Yellow	White	Black
Flavors	Sour	Bitter	Sweet	Acid	Salt
Organs	Liver	Heart	Spleen	Lung	Kidney
Sense Organs	Eye	Tongue	Mouth	Nose	Ear

By viewing our bodies as being made up of interconnected pieces—rather than organs functioning in a more singular, less related way—which is usual in Western medicine where we treat one organ for an illness—Chinese medicine always looks to treat the whole body. Knowledge of energy flow, of balance and imbalance, mutual creation and mutual destruction is examined in a very intricate, sophisticated theory that takes years to properly learn. This theory precisely explains how deficiency in one organ creates a malfunctioning of another, or of several other organs. Bringing balance to the dysfunctional organ restores balance in the whole body. This intricate system of rebalancing involves more than a quick bottle of medicine. Instead, it approaches the imbalance from a holistic perspective.

If we have a health problem, everything in life that we are affected by is analyzed from the perspective of our attitude toward an event and whether that attitude has balanced or unbalanced us. An inappropriate attitude is examined: What has its effect on the chi flow been? What imbalance was created? How can that particular balance be corrected?

By understanding the five elements and their flexible relationship to one another, a vast understanding of healing can be accomplished. The health problem is disclosed when the destructive interaction between any two elements is uncovered: various tools are then applied to create a balance and correct the problem at its source. These tools or methods include T'ai Chi, which fills the internal chi reservoirs; acupuncture and acupressure points to stimulate the meridians (chi highways throughout the body) and correct internal balances in the chi flow; herbs to bolster the body's reserves and give precisely intended nourishment where needed; and specific breathing instructions such as Qigong to aid in the cultivation of chi. Attitude adjustments are suggested. Arts, music, silence, and meditation are also part of a program for correcting illness and resuming a life of long health.

T'ai Chi and the Five Elements

Each step and hand movement of T'ai Chi is designed to put chi flows into accord with one another and the larger universal system of energy. Each T'ai Chi movement has been assigned an element.

A forward step .... Metal
A withdraw step .... Wood
Looking left .... Water
Looking right.................... Fire
Central equilibrium .... Earth

Chi—differentiated into yin and yang—permeates the five elements through a series of energy veins called meridians. There are twelve meridians that run throughout the body like energy highways. Each meridian is assigned to maintain a particular organ. The energy flow of the organ and the flow of the meridian are identical. So if the flow is off balance in the meridian, it is in the organ too.

> In this culture we rely so much on our mind we become separate from other aspects of our living.
> —Al Huang

The meridians pass through the entire body, head, trunk, arms, and legs. All along these pathways are points that respond to stimulation. These are precise locations that are used to regulate the energy flow and therefore correct dysfunction in the organ, correct the meridian system, and correct physical health.

These meridian pathways are identical in all people. So predictable is their placement that maps of their routes are common and used by students and masters alike. Illustrations of how these meridians look and where they are located on the body can be found in most books written on health from the Chinese perspective.

T'ai Chi promotes, nurtures, and maintains the unification of the body/mind/spirit. T'ai Chi also accomplishes something far more intricate. Each movement is precisely designed to affect yin-yang balance and to promote the correct energetic balance of the five elements to ensure organ health. This is probably why there are so many over-fifty people benefiting from T'ai Chi. As we get older we don't have automatic, easy access to youthful, high-energy chi. Staying healthy becomes an art. As chi fills our organs, joints, muscles, and bones through our practice, we can become healthier. As we function better, the natural pleasures in life—food, sleep, movement—are more accessible, thankfully. We can't take our body back in time, but we can get our organs to function at the best level they are capable of. And how will you ever know what can be accomplished unless you see for yourself how T'ai Chi and its surrounding influence can improve the quality of your life.

Part Two

Cultivating Your Own Practice

Chapter 4

Assessing Your Personal Needs

The term "older adult" encompasses a large and varied group. It loosely means fifty-year-olds—some barely feeling time passing in their bodies—to seniors, venerable folks in their eighties, nineties, and beyond who are well aware of the movement of time within their bodies. It is hard to see a strong common thread in a group that covers five decades, but there is an important common ground. This commonality usually starts slowly, and progresses, creating an increased awareness of and concern with the life of the body. Although aspects of youth and vitality can remain for decades (making our changing unique for each one of us), this process is at once predictable and unpredictable.

We have a fabulous array of tools available to improve and stabilize our health and well-being. In such a variety of choices the question becomes which choices are the wisest. What will support our life quality? What will maintain and even improve our quality of life for a very long time and fill in some areas of incomplete health now being found in the over-fifties?

These questions can be put off in youth. But when the knees twinge, the skin changes, the girth spreads, and breath becomes shorter, we are being offered an opportunity to actively patrol health and well-being options. This is perhaps why this book rests in your hands right now. Your curiosity brought you here and it is your curiosity about maturing well that will allow you to become fascinated with winding your way through this new world.

Personal Assessment

After she turned seventy, a wonderful woman, Be (not Bea but Be) set about the process of learning about aging and its joys and concerns. She had decided to turn her thoughts into a book. It was to be something like *The Measure of My Days* by Florida Scott Maxwell. She amassed information on traditional medical methods in geriatrics. She used her fabulous mind to explore the ever-expanding world of nutrition and alternative healthcare. She delved into meditation and studied it with great wonder. After five years of completely and thoroughly exploring the world available to the older adult, she wrote a 350-page manuscript. As she was on the verge of sending it in, she was quite suddenly filled with the simplicity of it all. She condensed her years of work into a few great lines.

> Enjoy the sunrise and count your blessings.
> Empty yourself each day.
> Live as if there is no tomorrow.
> Love as if there is only eternity.
> Find a doctor you love and trust.
> Eighty percent of your food good for you, twenty percent pure fun.
> Treasure your friends and family.
> Sleep deeply.

Be took her personal credo into her life and T'ai Chi became a morning meditation. On the hills overlooking the Pacific Ocean she practiced T'ai Chi with great satisfaction. One day a man came up to her. After watching until she was done, he asked if he could join in. Several mornings later his wife joined them. One by one, two by two, a whole group formed around Be. After a while they decided to get a teacher to come in occasionally to help the positioning. The teacher brought her skill and then joined in as well. I imagine they are still at it on the hill at sunrise, T'ai Chi-ing with the ocean's waves. We just never know where life is going to lead us!

Strategies like Be's are a good approach here—strategies for support, enhancement, and life improvement for your maturing body. Over our lifetime we have mapped out many strategies to create our life—career, family planning, financial planning, vacations, etc. Let's continue making a plan or a map for your journey now—whether it is just starting or has been going on for quite a while. This plan will look clearly at your knowledge about your own health and well-being and take into consideration the health history of your known family.

To get started, you might consider drawing up a list of the personal changes you are aware of, what you would like to effect, and the amount of focused time you would be willing to devote to this each day. Or perhaps you have already done a personal assessment and are now looking for time-efficient, effective answers to get on the top of this list or even get to a point where you can cross off each listed challenge as no longer problematic. T'ai Chi could very well be one of your better solutions.

Creating New Goals

As our moms and grannies said: An ounce of prevention is worth a pound of cure. T'ai Chi is the ounce of prevention that can reduce the heavy weight of a body becoming more burdensome and uncomfortable and the down feelings that most often accompany these developments.

No one wants to think that the process of senioring will produce discomfort and depression. But for many, this does happen. Knowing that this uncertainty lies with each person who embraces a long life, doesn't it make all the sense in the world to develop a strategy for all our years?

During earlier stages of our life when a new challenge presented itself, we stretched and mapped out a new, and hopefully appropriate, course. It is time that we do the same again. A growing amount of research and personal testimony attest to T'ai Chi being a viable contender for addition to this newly forged pathway. Here we are living in a time when science has brought us tools to improve the maturing of our body. New technology has relieved and extended the body's life as never before and yet it is an ancient tool from the past that ranks right up there at the top for enhancing all stages of life.

To start your new life plan, it may be helpful to create three lists: one on what you need to get by, one on what you need to be comfortable, and one on what you need to live a good life. This list of the three levels of self-care may prove to be not only a useful tool, but perhaps life changing, as it was for Kathy.

Kathy was born in the late 1940s and came into her adult life in the thrust of women's liberation. Newly filled with the desire to contribute with her life, she changed her major at her college from Art to Political Science with a minor in business. As our country settled down from the Vietnam War, she entered international business. Twenty years later she was successful and had a lifestyle many would love to have as their own. From the outside looking in, it appeared to be filled with travel, interesting people, fabulous cities, and a wealth of experiences. Eventually she married someone who was also in international business. Their life looked amazing.

But as Kathy entered her fifties, she became increasingly aware that somehow, in some mysterious way, she had lost track of herself in the fast pace of

Human anatomy is, of course, absolutely fundamental to an understanding of the human organism. We can only begin to know who we are once we understand *what* we are. While actual dissection is probably the most accurate instructive way to obtain an accurate knowledge of the human body, it isn't much help to artists, dancers, or other people who wish to know something about human anatomy but do not belong to a medical school, nor, in most cases, have any strong desire to examine dead bodies in detail. For such people, there are, however, many books, charts, drawings, and photographs that are almost as useful. The best known and most respected of all anatomical writings is *Gray's Anatomy*.

—Introduction to *Gray's Anatomy*

her life. Turning to T'ai Chi, she found a form of movement and exercise that could come with her and she could do it wherever she was staying. It seemed perfect. As she continued to deepen her practice, it began to become clear to her there were parts of herself that had submerged despite the great success in her chosen profession. It was not entirely clear to her what the longings consisted of, but it was clear they were deeply felt.

At about this time, she followed the suggestion of drawing up her three lists. She was amazed to find she had virtually no idea what the answers to the first list were, let alone the second and third. She knew discipline and commitment from years of work. She applied these now, and was able to ferret out the answers these simple lists were asking. It took time—and much trial and error and honing—to get the first one right, but when she did, the results were quite compelling. She discovered deep arenas of loneliness within, not because her life wasn't great, but because she had no concept of self-nurturing. As a result, she could not personally feast and be nourished deeply by her life. Her lack of self-nurturing skills made her Teflon-coated to the most personal pleasures of her life. By the time she finished the third list, she had honed her life to serve her in the most rewarding ways. Once starting down this path, she had no desire to return to a busy, exhausting venue. She kept her job, but she scaled it back. She reinvented herself by putting art from her own hand back into her life. Her friendships became deeper, and the ones that didn't just fell away. Her marriage took on that wonderful, smooth, well-kneaded quality that real marriages create over time. The life she had worked so hard to create now supported her in the ways that were most meaningful. From the outside looking in, her life still looked great, and now from the inside living it, it was truly great. Two simple tools—T'ai Chi and the self-nurturing test—were all it took.

> T'ai Chi needs commitment: The reward is in the commitment.

Here is an example of a plan. All you need to do is create three lists. Keep in mind that the necessities for a body-healthy life well lived are:

Great sleep
Meaningful exercise
Quiet, grateful thanks time
A diet compatible with your unique chemistry and food supplements
A trusted health practitioner
Friends
Family

List 1: What you need to just get by
1. The minimum number of hours of sleep you need
2. The minimum amount of exercise you need

3. Minimum quiet time for reflection
4. Minimum food for nourishment
5. Minimum time with a friend
6. Minimum time spent with family

List 2: Your comfortable list

1. Sleep you need to be comfortable and reasonably rested
2. The exercise you need to feel healthy.
3. Time for meaningful inner reflection
4. Kinds and frequency of food that is satisfying and the right supplements
5. Time spent with friends that is satisfying
6. Time with or speaking to family members that leaves you with a good feeling of blood connection

List 3: The optimum list for a good life

1. Ideal amount of sleep
2. Ideal amount and type of exercise
3. Perfect amount of inner reflection time
4. The best nutrition and supplementation for the health of your body
5. Wonderful and full time spent with friend or friends
6. Meaningful time with your family

Now that you have the three lists compiled with a combination of self-knowing, educated guesses, and probably some blind stabs in the dark, let's return to the first list.

Check to make sure you still agree essentially with what you have. Spend a week watching how well you are doing at getting the minimum you need. You may be shocked to see that on this minimal list your basic health and well-being needs aren't being regularly met. Begin to upgrade your self-care to meet the minimum list. And. . .add T'ai Chi in as the activity.

For the first list, do three T'ai Chi warm-ups each day. That's all. You can do the same three or vary them. Get the rest of your life up to meet that minimum list. Doing the beginning warm-ups of T'ai Chi will help give you a sense of progressing in your learning. Then after you have this first list well in place, pull out the second list. You might need to revise it some because you know a bit more about yourself from completing the first list. T'ai Chi can continue to support your upgrading here. Add in three more warm-ups. As you move to satisfy your self-designed list, T'ai Chi will help give you your desired increased energy, greater ability to relax, sharper and clearer appetite, and an increased optimism toward life and people in general.

Is it important to do this type of an upgrade as you start T'ai Chi? Only if you are really ready to take a step forward in your commitment to prevention and health and well-being maintenance. T'ai Chi will affect you in any state of health and it will improve you in many ways, as previously stated. T'ai Chi has no requirements for entry and is limitless in where it can assist and support you. You can join your practice into a planned strategy for health enhancement and as a result increase the initial benefits as well as the long-term ones.

Committing to T'ai Chi

The Chinese say that anyone who practices T'ai Chi with regularity will gain the pliability of a child, the vitality of a lumberjack, and the peace of mind of a sage. These become the very goals that we seek throughout our life, but they become particularly cherished qualities in our after-fifty years—to be supple, strong, and vitally alive. For rewards as rich and plentiful as these, some discipline and effort seem worthwhile.

As you learn T'ai Chi it will become natural for you to relax into your center—the tan t'ien. This, in turn, creates a deep feeling of relaxed ease within. You will also be connecting your thoughts into your movements, directing your actions with your mind. This is the absolute opposite of action through habit.

It is amazing watching the focused concentration, presence, and excitement of discovery as a child learns. This is because it is all new for them. So to get it, they need to be fully into it—body, mind, and emotions all there, everything fully absorbed and engaged in the experience. We begin to give up this state of full presence as we get older and our life of learned habits and beliefs take over. We get rhythms we are comfortable with. We move our bodies in predictably repetitive ways, developing patterns of movement that identify us as accurately as our voice. Generally, the older we get, the more habitual we become. Those comfort zones we have worked so hard for feel good, as they should. But we also develop habits that actually promote less alert attentiveness and presence in our daily life.

And why would this be a problem? The nervous system thrives on variety—not overload or sameness, but variety. The nervous system, like a child, loves to have new experiences to rise to the fun of learning. Over time, with our tendency toward predictability and habits, we decrease our desire for the new and increased variety. This variety, generally brought to us by children, occurs less often. Children draw us into life as it is. The responsibilities we took on that also drew us into the stimulation and variety of life have generally diminished. This can be wonderful, as it can facilitate free time to do as we choose. But there is a tricky balance between living the golden years by becoming more engaged with life as it is or becoming more and more limited to our habits and comfort zone. The ideal is to take the ongoing experiences of life and become more flexible, understanding, and wise. Maturing is the precious gift of living because the experiences of our life bring us an accumulation of achievements and self-knowledge. It is this hard-won self-knowledge that has given us the ability to create comfort for ourselves. But the caveat is finding a new, truly new, fresh stimulation and, even more importantly, being able to engage with a new, fresh, and excited attitude, like a child. To not solve this dilemma leads inevitably to feeling old, out of touch, passed by.

This delicate balance between comfort and challenge can be found through dedicated practice of T'ai Chi. Through this kind of attained unique movement, we can truly encourage the consistent health and vitality we crave and long to maintain. As you become suppler, stronger, and better oxygenated your pleasure in life will increase. You become more easily flexible, centered, confident, and fresh. Your normal body movement will echo the wisdom of the effects of T'ai Chi practice. As the body, so the mind. The unique value of T'ai Chi is that the discipline offers a rare opportunity to blend your body's movement, your thoughts, and your feeling nature. Each affects the others, and the outcome of this balanced blending is inner peace.

It is from this gentle alignment of body and mind that the improved state of well-being, the wonder of T'ai Chi, emanates. Gone are the days, for most of us, when body and mind aligned naturally in a common activity. The world of the child's delight in one activity is generally lost to us through our multi-layered living, the body does one thing while the mind does another. The body sits passively while the mind actively engages a book, and we watch birds as we rake leaves, we wonder about a friend as we drive home, all the while relying on a combination of body habits, unconscious memory, and an active mind to keep us upright and moving forward. This produces more problems than anyone could shake a stick at. Stress is the convenient umbrella term that identifies a myriad of discomforts emanating from this single cause.

T'ai Chi offers one of the few activities in our Western world today that put the movement of the body, the commands of the mind, and the current feeling state all together in one delightful experience. Of course, it is only after experiencing the meaningful improvements T'ai Chi has brought to you that this becomes a reality.

T'ai Chi is really a come-as-you-are party. When you make the decision to go forward, then do it with a commitment to avoid at all costs self-deprecation

The theories on the beginnings of T'ai Chi Chuan have varied so much that an effort to trace T'ai Chi Chuan and Qigong back in time was started by researcher Tang Hao in 1932. In his extensive research he questioned deeply that Chang San-feng was the originator. His research found that a more probable beginning was in the Ming Dynasty. General Chi Chi-Kuang, a great national hero of his time, had put together sixteen martial art practices. He appeared to pick the most outstanding sixteen and then summarized them and systematized them. After coming to this conclusion, Tang's final analysis was that T'ai Chi Chuan was born of the people of China, that it has its origins in the people and had been incorporated into the art of martial arts over time.

and self-criticism. Go to T'ai Chi to accept. However you do it, it's fine. Practice the warm-ups and postures in this book. When you feel a smidgeon closer to understanding, then find a class. Go open. Go receptive. Leave satisfied with yourself. Practice to reap more benefits.

Chapter 5

Setting the Right Environment for Success

We have a pretty impatient culture. Multi-tasking, volumes of information, scads of people rushing by, and many efficient machines do tasks so well that we need to do our own faster. This provides a peculiar foundation for accomplishment in T'ai Chi. While T'ai Chi is meant to be an experience, we Westerners rush in wanting to get it now. While T'ai Chi gently unfolds, we want the benefits to present themselves now. While time pushes on, the demand for T'ai Chi to step up to the plate and show its worth soon is intense. This creates a pretty unpleasant environment of internal impatience. Couple this impatience with a difficulty in remembering the positions and their connecting motions, and we have a perfect recipe for frustration and giving up.

Every T'ai Chi student wants to get it more quickly, would love to step into the practice more deeply, would love to move in one steady, rhythmic flow from beginning to end. In order to accomplish this, four important steps are valuable.

1. Accept your pace of learning
2. Develop a learner's attitude
3. Find a great instructor
4. Create a good T'ai Chi/Qigong space

Accept Your Own Pace of Learning

The first, accepting your own pace of learning, is the most essential. Without this personal acceptance, nothing else can really occur. The pace at which you learn is perfect for you. It stimulates your nervous system exactly as you need it. Your pace tones your muscles exactly as they need to be toned and balanced to assure that your unique body alignment improves over time. Your learning pace *is* you. T'ai Chi has no demand for speed—actually, it is better done very slowly. T'ai Chi has no time limit you must reach before you achieve benefit—the benefit starts immediately. T'ai Chi has no foundation of competition—it is truly an exercise of equals—with no built-in competition. Appreciate the skill of others, but don't compete. T'ai Chi is many, many things, but one thing it absolutely is not, is competitive. T'ai Chi has and does belong to millions—and it is also most personally yours.

If you find T'ai Chi is right for you and you are determined to pursue and learn its sequential movements successfully, then two words tie you to every T'ai Chi Ch'uan or T'ai Chi practitioner: Do it. This is the most often repeated suggestion down through the centuries: Do it. Do it. Do it. Make it your commitment. Set aside the time each day. Have a consistent space to use. It is like any close relationship: Give it time, space, and commitment, and it will gently, over time, unfold its treasures within you. Don't let fatigue, stiffness, or passivity stand in your way. It doesn't matter how stiff, tired, etc. you are. T'ai Chi will meet you right where you are. So just do it. Do your best and bless the rest.

The primary quandary that accompanies learning T'ai Chi is: What follows this, where to now? The question of remembering sequences can loom large in the mind of anyone who wants to get the entire piece down pat.

Committing the sequences to memory is a bit of a challenge for any student, and there is no doubt that coming near the desired quality is more elusive when we have passed our fiftieth year. The teacher may look as light as a feather and graceful as sea grass, and you may feel as if you are just feeling your way along. From one practice to another your mind may be dominated by thoughts of the next sequence, your foot placement, remembering whether the stance is a thirty percent-seventy percent or if your left leg should be empty/yin. It does not matter! It truly is a self-made problem. (If you have a teacher who makes it a problem, or

---

A Guide List
In finding your perfect instructor, remember:
- Find a yang form class. There may be variations in the yang short form. These minor variations make little difference.
- Set your own pace.
- Observe the teacher's T'ai Chi .
- Do you like the teacher's movements?
- Do you feel relaxed enough in their presence to learn from them?
- Is the class well planned? (See "Picking a Good Class Format.")
- Is the class taught in a clear supportive style?
- Is the instructor interested in and attentive to any health concerns you may have?
- Is the room well lit, spacious, and filled with fresh air?
- Is there a time of quiet centering at the beginning of class and relaxation at the end?
- Are the fees for the class reasonable?

worse, an embarrassment, dump 'em.) At the top of the list of things to remember is this: You are gaining from the process.

The trick with the starting point for T'ai Chi is to start. Just start. Let the process of learning be the only goal. Your muscle memory will build. When this happens, you won't need to think about each and every muscle. Your muscles will remember on their own as you repeat the movements, and then, one fine day what you have been working on will just be there. This new, most effortless approach to moving will filter into your body. Not just through T'ai Chi alone, you will move with greater comfort and flexibility in all movements. Ease of motion will become happily a part of everyday life. At this point, practice will take on a whole new dimension. How long will it take? Your integration of T'ai Chi will happen in sections completely appropriate to your own timing. To get a general idea, look to the past and see basically how learning physically and/or mentally has been for you before. This will give you a general guideline of your own unique timing.

Develop a Learner's Attitude

In ancient China T'ai Chi Ch'uan was taught through secret transmission. The only way to learn it was to be one of the chosen few. Often chosen as children, their entire focus was on T'ai Chi Ch'uan. The student would be disciplined in studies, practice, competition, arts, and meditation. He would become a master known throughout the country and an undying legend living beyond his time.

It was with this knowledge the young student entered his first training session. His entrance was filled with gratitude and wonder at what he would learn. He was also imbued with the spirit of honoring both his mentor and the T'ai Chi Ch'uan discipline that would so deeply affect his life. Both master and student came together with high hopes for a successful outcome and a mutual honoring for the service they were about to impart to each other—the master's skill in exchange for the furthering of the lineage they both held so important. This all transpired before the very first instruction or transmission. Mutual respect, a passion for the endeavor, a reverence for the lineage, and a longing for warrior skills and spiritual attunement converged to create the best possible attitude for attentive learning and disciplined practice.

This is the learner's attitude that we should bring to our T'ai Chi practice. You can greatly enhance your own learning by embracing this respect, passion, reverence, and longing: Remember with respect all who have gone before you. Recognize what an enormous asset to health and well-being T'ai Chi is. When you arrive at class, you will be unlocking the gifts T'ai Chi has retained for you.

Learning over Fifty

For most of us senior moments (a rather indelicate term) are now a fact of life. Few students over fifty don't experience them. Since they are a part of our life, we have two reactions to choose from: to avoid them by resenting the moments, denying them, and closing down to life one situation at a time; or to accept them by adapting to them and going on with life. Life is always full and rich. The only requirement is to engage it. So the obvious solution to those moments is to adapt and be patient. As Katherine Hepburn said, "keep on a-goin', you'll get there."

What you will probably notice when you begin practicing is that over time our bodies have developed movement habits. When someone is at a distance and you can't yet quite make out who it is, it will be the unique pattern of their movement that will first identify them. These body habits are as unique as our face, but they are not always in our best interest. Often these are areas of chronic tension—tension that can come from long-term stress. This kind of stress is interesting because these areas of chronic holding can come from early childhood issues and still be held within. For instance, if a child had a critical parent, he would raise the shoulders and indent the chest at the sternum. If the criticism kept up long enough, these tension patterns stay. They may be old and familiar, but they are certainly not assisting our health and well-being. T'ai Chi will begin to return elasticity to these areas. The emotion that has held the muscles in this tension for all those decades, releases and the sense of health and well-being that is our birthright is restored.

Tension can also build up around a body injury. This tension can exceed what is necessary to stabilize the area and begin to impede ease of movement. Everyone has been loaded with these tensions.

Even if there has been judicious attention paid to easing the imbalances, they still often arise under returning stress. These stress-holding habits are familiar and easy to overlook, until they begin to bother us. A twinge, a hip glitch, a rigid back, stiff neck. . .the list goes on and on. These symptoms are beckoning us toward T'ai Chi and Qigong. Instead of choosing to step into denial—"I've always moved this way," "Why should I change?" "I don't need fixing!"—with its long-term consequences, choose to interface with the body challenge. Become curious and actively alive to this part of life. What works? Is there a way to feel better? If so, what is it? Stay engaged with each step of life as it progresses.

> Rejuvenate—
> make your life
> a spring of eternity.

You will find that this one form of movement, T'ai Chi, supports finding comfort while engaging in life as it presents itself. It teaches us when to step forward and be strong (yang). It teaches when to step back and be quiet (yin). It bolsters the internal world so a feeling of being fortified and confident is present. It teaches about releasing and letting go. Managing disappointing loss and grief is an important tool to learn. T'ai Chi teaches opening and fully engaging what is being brought to us by life and the moment. It is quite a wonderful experience to learn life skills of such paramount importance through a movement that also heals and balances the body.

There are three levels of instruction—teaching, coaching, and training. You need all three to learn good T'ai Chi.

Teaching is where things are explained to a whole class at a time, and each person goes off alone or works with others (in the case of push-hands) to incorporate the instructions into their form, their bodies, the art.

Coaching is where the instructor works with you specifically and says something like, "Go home and practice this week, this is what you are trying to do, this is how it will feel, and come back and show me what you learned, and tell me how it felt."

Training is where the instructor is with you and says something like, "This is what is going on here, try it… What does it feel like? No, try this…. Look for this feeling…. Try it again…. That is closer…. That's right…. Now go home and practice and we will build on it next week."

—http://lifematters.com/taiteach.html (3/9/2001)

Embrace a learner's attitude—one that encourages a healthy life—and you will go far in your T'ai Chi practice.

Find a Great Instructor

At some point after picking up this book you will be ready for instruction from a teacher. Books and videos are great for initial familiarity, but at some point a real live teacher becomes essential. You will know when the time is right—it could be immediately or down the road. As you follow the book's instructions, warm-ups, and initial T'ai Chi and Qigong steps, you will already feel progress. At some point enhancing this process will make all the sense in the world.

The right T'ai Chi teacher is a wonderful find. You may live in an area where there is only one or two, or perhaps none. Or you may be in a larger area where T'ai Chi teachers abound. No matter. If you are unable to locate a teacher near you, then get a few good videos. You can also subscribe to a T'ai Chi magazine or sign up for one of the intensive camps that advertise there. These camps are great for everyone, but can become essential for the lone learner.

Here are some tips that might help you to select a video:

- Find an instructor who is middle-aged or beyond. You will benefit from their empathetic, seasoned approach, and it may mean they have been doing T'ai Chi for a longer time.
- Find a tape—a beginner level is nice—teaching the yang short form so it is consistent with the book and your class.
- Make sure they combine instruction for both movement and breath.
- Make sure the voice of the video teacher doesn't grate on you.

- You may have a video rental store where you can try out several different videos. This will give you a good feel for what type of video you like. Usually you can find an assortment of approaches to Qigong as well.

If there are teachers in your area, it is important to find the teacher that is right for you and your personal needs and tastes. Here are some tips that might help you select a teacher:

- Your teacher should be calm and relaxed. When your teacher moves, it will look as though every part of the body is at ease. The movements will be light and fluid.
- Your teacher should have mind and body linked as they do the T'ai Chi movements. This link leads to a sense of them being very present both in the T'ai Chi action and in their contact with you.
- Your teacher should have humility. T'ai Chi is not competitive like T'ai Chi Ch'uan. The established environment for learning T'ai Chi is sharing a form together. The teacher is a guide. A T'ai Chi teacher that needs to be the best can create a weird competition with other teachers or even students. The need to be the center, special, or the best person can interfere with excellent T'ai Chi instruction.
- A true teacher teaches because of a deep love for T'ai Chi. The slow, even movements are done in a manner of grace and sharing. The teacher is not seeking adulation or fawning devotion.
- Your teacher should have a clear understanding of how to demonstrate each position and an ability to talk it through, and keep an eye on students is essential. Shoulders are relaxed. Arms hang in a relaxed manner. Elbows, pointed down, never lead the movement. The body weight will be balanced and in a straight line. The root will be firmly positioned in only one foot at a time as the motions progress.
- It is desirable to learn from someone who is also always learning. Seminars, classes, and even traveling to expand their own skill are good signs.
- The teacher should encourage natural, slow, and deepening breath. There should be a good working knowledge of how the movements and breath correlate and also a repertoire of breath exercises—Qigong. T'ai Chi movement cannot fulfill itself without these breathing skills.
- It is important that you are able to observe the class to get a feel for it. You should feel comfortable about asking questions.
- Your teacher should recognize that early learning is the most demanding and provide an environment of patience, enthusiasm, and support. The development of these essential skills is most evident when the teacher is working with a slow learner. Each student is honored. No self-esteem is bruised or compromised.

- Your teacher should provide a great breadth of interest in student diversity. T'ai Chi has been enhanced by every person who has attended to it. This is true for you, too. You will have your own way of yielding to the form and expressing it.
- Instruction should be clear and repeated as often as necessary. A flexible, adaptive instructor who understands the memory demands of T'ai Chi is significant. An instructor who sees small gains as large triumphs is a treasure. Too many people have become too frustrated with learning because of the teacher's lack of patience. A teacher dedicated to the process and who values the effort as the goal is essential.
- It is great to find a teacher who has a great breadth of knowledge of both T'ai Chi and Qigong. It adds to the interest and fun.
- T'ai Chi and Qigong are going through a great transition as they race around the world. In a state of flux such as this, it is wonderful to have a teacher who embraces the expansion as opposed to one who is critical of other teachers, forms, and schools.

> Do nothing but needlework
> I remain with my eyes
> Focused on a single spot
> And this is the way.
> —Ainu saying
> *Songs of Humans, Songs of Gods*

- Do you have a physical limit? Has your doctor okayed T'ai Chi for you? Share your limits with your teacher. Does the teacher listen with attentive interest? Are there creative ideas for adapting the movement to your need?
- Is your teacher available for private instruction? T'ai Chi and Qigong require no one but you to do them. They aren't necessarily partnership or group activities. Many people stick to the traditional mode of teaching—one-to-one instruction. If you can find and afford such instruction, it is probably the best.

Create a Good T'ai Chi/Qigong Space

Since the primary requisites for T'ai Chi are you, your self-determination, and a very good instructor, you are already two-thirds of the way there. The last thing you need is a good place to practice.

Creating the Right Home Environment

If you are practicing at home, it is important that you have a quiet space that you can go to that is free from clutter and large enough for you to move around in. Pick a place where you will be free from any disruption—the television, the computer, the phone, and so on. Make sure you feel safe and comfortable in your practice area. Here are some tips on preparing your space:

- Create a space for T'ai Chi to thrive. This space can be visual or audio, it can be a space in a room, or a time space. It can be shaped only by your intent to enter into the form or it can be a space you create with sound, physical placement, and so on. There are many ways to create and shape a space away from a class.
- If you are going to do T'ai Chi with another person, keep the conversation limited. A brief greeting on meeting and then a silent, warm parting is appropriate. This is a lovely way to ordain a time space filled only with T'ai Chi movement. The silence between you creates the space.
- Nature was the original inspiration for T'ai Chi and practicing T'ai Chi in a natural environment, or in front of a window, can inspire you to move with the lightness of a leaf in the wind, the steady step of an animal walking by, the quiet stretching upward of a tree, or the gentle swaying of a flower. Zhang San Feng found T'ai Chi Ch'uan in these interactions; you will find T'ai Chi there as well. Let the movement of nature around you seep into your form. Do it for you. Make it a personal, very personal, interactive venture.
- Create predictable silence by turning off your phones, even your cell phone. T'ai Chi thrives as you acquiesce to silence.
- Use your imagination to create a protective screen around your space, a chi screen put there through your intent. Make your space as cozy or expanded as you wish. Some people like to imagine a shape like a large egg surrounding them about arm's length away, as if you have slipped into a large, flexible, egg-like chi container. You can make it any size and color you want. This can enhance a space of calm and inner attunement in any environment you might be in. Imagine when you walk into the center of this egg that the surface is actually screening out of you all concerns, so as you enter the egg, you leave your concerns outside and do your form. Then, when you decide to step out of the egg, your concerns can congregate around you again. But what you may find is that after your T'ai Chi break they are a bit more distant. You may feel you have more inner freedom and peace, and this will have a positive effect on how you handle your concerns as you step back into real time.
- Playing an audio tape of music you love sets a wonderful studio space.
- Following a video teacher's instructions also creates a space. You will need to watch at the start of your learning, but as you progress with your skill and confidence, you will find listening to the verbal instructions enough. Then when you do feel unsure, you have the video right there to check in with.
- Create a classic space with a small cup of green tea. What a marvelous leaf green tea is made from. Long used in China and Japan ceremonially, it peps you up with a bit of caffeine and also opens up your breathing. It

is a great little addition to your morning and a lovely precursor to T'ai Chi practice.

- Is doing T'ai Chi getting a bit stale? Is it losing some of its fun? Remember, the nervous system loves variety, so alter your space or actually change to another space periodically. Each spot you choose will have its own effect on your T'ai Chi.

Balancing your Space with Feng Shui

There are other steps you can take to actually design a physical space in which to practice T'ai Chi. The design format that is the most congruent with T'ai Chi is *Feng Shui* (pronounced FEN SCHWAY). Feng Shui is the ancient art of placement to create balance and harmony. The Chinese approach to placement acknowledges that chi is an all-encompassing source of life. When we understand that chi responds to contours and shapes of a room—as well as beams of light, breezes, mirrors, windows, and the placement of all objects in an environment—we can design our space to promote optimal chi flow.

If you ever have the opportunity to enter a home or room architecturally designed and then decorated with Feng Shui principles, you will sense a rare peace, harmony, and easy vitality within the confines of the space. This environment of peace and harmony is the perfect atmosphere in which to live and also to do T'ai Chi.

When the Feng Shui is correct, the environment is in balance—it is already in that instant of T'ai Chi when the Wu Chi flows forth into life. The exquisite chi wisdom of the ancient Chinese unfolded the secrets of the not often seen, but always felt, chi world that underlies and permeates our physical world. T'ai Chi and Feng Shui were created to harvest this eternal gift of life for the good of human kind.

Creating harmony in your environment will promote inner balance, it will reduce stress, it slows early aging, and it allows youthful vitality to flow through your body. The aim of doing T'ai Chi in a Feng Shui environment is to place yourself so you are a part of the art of placement. Design your space so you are in the center. Have all of the surrounding environment support you. As you discover your Feng Shui possibilities and step into your T'ai Chi form within this exquisite balance, much of life's weight will be lifted from you.

Choosing the Right Class Environment

If you are practicing in a class, here are some things to look out for:

- Small Classes: This is a good option for both the student and teacher. A few people working together in a roomy, light space can accomplish a lot.
- Large Classes: These are generally not ideal, but if the instructor has assistants helping and if you can see easily, it can be workable and is usually the most affordable way to learn.

Another great side effect of T'ai Chi is the friends you will make. Unlike T'ai Chi Ch'uan of old, where one to one was the teaching style, T'ai Chi is taught in the West in classes. The ambiance of the class, if in keeping with the art, will be peaceful, supportive, and encouraging. Often after class or during the week there are opportunities to get together with a few class members and work on the movements together. Friendship is the heartbeat of life and everyone needs friendship with which to share life's pleasure.

To begin T'ai Chi, it is generally best to enter a class that is starting a new cycle of learning, as opposed to entering an ongoing class. The beginning class can be demanding and it usually is easier if everyone is at the same point. This beginning class will focus on the foundation of the form and special terminology will be introduced. Foundation of the form consists of basic stances and movements and initial breath work. Here are some other things to look for in choosing a class:

Picking a Good Class Format

- Pleasing space
- Silent at the beginning
- Brief, effective warm-up
- A demonstration of what has been learned
- Name and explanation of what is to be added
- Clear demonstration, with new steps taught in a uniform manner
- Students are led into a new step, breaking it up in manageable pieces as necessary. Repeat the new step.
- Start the positions from the top, naming each one (It helps with memory!)
- Reviewing and adding in new steps
- A quiet time integrating the learned steps with the new. This encourages the mind and body to engage.
- Verbal instruction is only what is necessary and is given in a rhythmic flow with the movements.
- Classes run about forty-five minutes
- Class focuses on tools for success: Correct teaching, personal perseverance, interest in the movement. Of these three, correct teaching is the most important.

Push-hands

Push-hands is a very interesting and important aspect of T'ai Chi. What makes this form so extraordinary is that in a class environment it will expose practitioners to a variety of people, and therefore, chi.

To practice Push-hands two people already familiar and comfortable with T'ai Chi stand opposite each other. The partners join their hands and follow their teacher's instructions.

Some believe that Push-hands is best put off until the foundation of co-existing yin-yang within a practitioner is firmly in place. When this container of yin and yang is well in place, and the flows of chi have been experienced within, then it is time to advance in your T'ai Chi practice. The practice of Push-hands is essential to fully develop as a T'ai Chi student.

Chapter 6

Your Own
T'ai Chi Practice

We've used the word "practice" a lot through this book but what does this really mean? We understand the verb "to practice" means "to prepare oneself"; it is also often used to refer to the value of repetition in order to come to a full understanding of something some time in the future. But this understanding of practice completely misses the point and value of T'ai Chi and Qigong. Though the process of repetition and refinement are essential assets to T'ai Chi as well as Qigong the value is really in the action itself—the process.

To practice T'ai Chi is to command your body to produce movement. It is also to command your body to produce a movement that is in agreement, harmony, and unanimity with your mind and spirit. This is the essence of T'ai Chi. If T'ai Chi teaches us one thing (and of course it doesn't—it teaches us many things), it teaches satisfaction in the present moment. There is nothing in T'ai Chi that calls you to perform in any way. There is nothing in T'ai Chi that demands a goal or a deadline for your learning. There is nothing in T'ai Chi but movement, space, and you.

You will hear the word "practice" used over and over again in this book; just remember what is really meant—that you command your body to produce T'ai Chi in agreement with you. To take this attitude of appreciation of the process into your integration of T'ai Chi will bring you much more deeply into what the form is all about for you. There is no authority higher than you when you are learning T'ai Chi—there are fabulous teachers from whom you can learn to refine your T'ai Chi but the key is to stay completely in agreement with yourself. If you do this, the movements of T'ai Chi and Qigong will have a far deeper and more gratifying effect on you and your life.

Most of the learning in our culture is a process that moves toward a definite goal. Very little of our learning has to do with a natural unfolding. Yet this is what T'ai Chi and Qigong offer, a process of movement that requires only one thing—you.

Your Own Practice

It is possible to feel a bit overwhelmed by T'ai Chi without this understanding of practice firmly entrenched—it is all too easy to become impatient with your progress. As a T'ai Chi participant, doing T'ai Chi means just one important thing: that you are practicing T'ai Chi for yourself, to improve the quality of your life, and you are practicing it for one reason—you have chosen it.

In your practice of T'ai Chi it is useful to find common ground with other T'ai Chi doers who have preceded your endeavors. Reflections from those who precede you can inspire very minor changes that can produce a whole host of deepening satisfaction with your own practice—done by you, done for you, and done at your own pace. Here is a selection of wise reflections from others.

Tips on Preparing Your Mind

- Arrange your thinking about T'ai Chi in such a way that you hold it in a special place. For example: You have a hard day or a stressful conversation, bad news from your broker or bank, the car breaks down, and so on. Train yourself to say, "Thank goodness I can do T'ai Chi later. I can't wait to relax into my form," "I am so grateful I can do T'ai Chi tonight and improve my mood." Purposely create an attitude of anticipation.

- Practice alone when you feel like it and with a companion when that seems like a better approach. Both will offer you a good environment for the movement to flourish.

- Start your T'ai Chi with a quiet moment of thanks for the lineage of skilled masters who crafted T'ai Chi Ch'uan, now sculpted into T'ai Chi, one person at a time. It is here for you because of their love and zeal.

- Before or after practice sit quietly with a book that quiets you, even inspires you. It can be a favorite on T'ai Chi, or any book that stills those thoughts and quiets the noisy emotions.

- Take a mini mental break before your practice. Close your eyes and bring to mind a lovely little corner of the world that you just love. Let this place return to all your senses. When you are filled with it, step into your form.

"The source of intention is in the waist." When the waist is relaxed and unfolding, it not only allows the chi to sink downward more easily, making turning and moving swift and agile, but it also makes the lower part become stronger and more solid. Avoid the problem of being heavy on the upper part and light on the lower part.

—Grandmaster Wu Chien-Ch'uan

Tips on Preparing Your Body

You have in the ankles and hands chi points called "gates." Giving these points a gentle massage can help enhance T'ai Chi by opening up the earth flow in the feet and the heavenly flow at the hand.

To find the point at your feet, place your finger in the space between the base of your big toe and the base of toe next to it. Slide your finger up your foot from this point. Just before you get to the crest of the foot, your finger will find a little dent that fits it perfectly. Rub in small, counterclockwise circles on the tops of both feet. These points release the upper chi flow into the body.

To find the hand point, lay your thumb across its same hand. There will be a crease in the skin as the thumb lies against the pointer finger. Massage the inception point of the crease, release your thumb and stretch the thumb and fingers out and apart. Some people pinch this point from both sides using the thumb and the pointer finger from the other hand. This point releases the downward flow of chi in the body.

> To integrate the lively energy from heaven and earth: This has always been the primary intent behind doing T'ai Chi and Qigong.

> Benevolence in T'ai Chi: Never try to harm anyone in practice, teaching, or demonstration. In T'ai Chi, you are competing with no one except yourself. If you feel a need to outdo your classmates in practice, then your real need is to overpower your own ego.
> —William C. Phillip, founder of Patience T'ai Chi Association

OTHER WAYS TO PREPARE YOUR BODY

- Find some aroma that you love. Rub it into the soles of your feet and then tap the soles of your feet with the tips of your fingers and fingernails.
- Take off your jewelry. All jewelry alters the flow of chi and it is ideal to be jewel- and metal-free as you do your T'ai Chi. Most especially, remove any watches or time pieces.
- Practice when you are more hungry than full.
- Practice with your belly relaxed, even rounded out.
- Practice at a time of day when your energy level is a bit low. You will feel a lift.
- Use T'ai Chi to help break a habit that you are tired of but can't quite stop. You will find that after T'ai Chi the desire will be diminished. "I will have that piece of cake after T'ai Chi." "I will worry about this and that after T'ai Chi." It will give you a nice little break between desire and fulfillment.
- Try T'ai Chi after a shower. When your skin is moist (but your feet are dry and secure!). As you do your form with a minimum of clothes, or none at all, you will feel very vivified by the cool breeze on your skin as you move and breathe through the form.

Bring Your Practice into Your Everyday Life

As you deepen your commitment to T'ai Chi, you may find yourself transferring the peace and harmony of your T'ai Chi practice into your daily actions. This occurs for a variety of reasons—a fascinating one is the gentle dissolving of our body habits.

Our lives are powerfully influenced by our body habits. These habits can turn food into self-nurturing, can turn a movie into a treasured memory, can turn a song into reverie. Our bodies are filled with habits based on memories of events no longer happening.

> Sink the chi to the tan t'ien.

> Tranquility is a way of developing vigilant attention.

As we get older, our health margin can narrow and we should all be looking to replace our outdated body habits with new, up-to-date ones—habits to replace overeating, chronic tension, nerves, low energy—that completely support our improving life.

It takes about six weeks of commitment to T'ai Chi in order for our bodies to recognize it as a new habit. After the nervous system begins the new wiring and the muscles get a bit of memory storing up, then you will be over the first big hump in your T'ai Chi practice. This is when your habit will start to give you significant support for doing T'ai Chi each day. T'ai Chi is pleasurable, comfortable, life enhancing, and sensuous—all attributes the body loves.

After the initial six to eight weeks of effort, it will start to settle in to your life, and a new refreshing aspect will become apparent to you. These are the mini-breaks that will start to pepper your day. These mini-breaks won't occur in the pre-designated time periods when T'ai Chi is being done in full form, instead, these are moments, experiences, and pauses in your everyday life where T'ai Chi gently asserts itself. It is a reservoir of calm that you can draw from. The bridges to this reservoir of inner calm are singular aspects of T'ai Chi and Qigong. Here are some examples:

- A pre-birth breath when traffic has jammed
- A gently lifted T'ai Chi hand at a time when inner grace needs to be accessed
- A T'ai Chi balance when your feet are sore, or your back hurts, or you're just standing and waiting
- A head evolving upward, shoulders relaxed, when you feel a headache coming on or muscles getting tense

These are some of the obvious mini T'ai Chi breaks. You will find many more. They may be new ease of movement, lightness, and sure-footedness in your step or a deepening capacity to take in oxygen. You may feel a steady increase in your sensual/sexual energy as the tan t'ien enlivens. These are all mini-breaks of pleasure that become welcome intrusions into your life. As these become manifold, a sense of deep dynamic relaxation will abound, and then all of this circles back to doing T'ai Chi. Your form becomes more meaningful. Your T'ai Chi ceases to be a discipline you are imposing upon yourself and becomes a body habit that combines with a life of increasing pleasure.

As your body incorporates the chi through your breath and movement, your habitual attitudes will update. No longer given to responding habitually, you find fresh attitudes, perceptions, and points of view unfolding. This is a symptom of presence—the ability to respond not habitually, but appropriately in any given situation.

T'ai Chi practice will bring many wonderful gifts of health and well-being into your life. Just keep these four touchstones in mind and your T'ai Chi will become more and more refined:

1. Take the time: Each day find the time to practice
2. Be patient: Allow your rhythm of learning to lead you
3. Be consistent: Regular practice is very important
4. Show up: Be present in the form

Part Three

Building a Foundation
for Your T'ai Chi Practice

Chapter 7

Breath—Life's Elixir

Breath is so cherished for what it carries to us that a whole philosophy of life springs from its vital well. It is this philosophy of life that is the central point in the Chinese approach to health. The Chinese believed our capacity for breath to be the very center of excellent health and satisfying longevity.

As humans, we internalize chi through breathing. Deep breath, more chi; shallow breath, less chi. The exultation of chi and its critical place in the maintenance of vitality led to great interest in methods for increasing its intake and cultivating it for maximum benefit.

It is this determined desire that led to the embrace of T'ai Chi Ch'uan and its sibling—Qigong (pronounced KEY GONG). Qigong is probably older than T'ai Chi Ch'uan, and its entire focus is breath empowerment with minimal motion. It was natural for the two to be crafted together.

Chi not only fills the lungs upon inhale, but it also fills and empowers everything else. Skin, organs, bones, joints, and circulation all are dependent on chi for health and to uphold appropriate function. It is for this reason T'ai Chi and Qigong become so effective.

Here are some breath exercises that are essential to your T'ai Chi practice.

Tan T'ien Tai Chi Breath in Three Steps

T'ai Chi breath is your most natural, most relaxed breath. Slow, relaxed, and gentle, it glides into your lungs in a way that your lung capacity increases, the organs lift and aerate, and the body heaves a sigh of relief as oxygen courses throughout. Chi sinks to the tan t'ien as oxygen fills the lungs. This is the deep and full breath of normal sleep. Breathing through the nose is the norm.

Step One

As your breath streams into your lungs, relax your abdomen and let the chi expand into the tan t'ien. Breathe into your expanding lungs and expanding abdomen. Then instead of actually focusing on the exhale, just relax. As you relax, the breath will flow out, the lungs and abdomen will relax. Try it again: Inhale, abdomen rounds out, lungs lift; relax, and out it flows. Again, abdomen rounds out, lungs lift and fill; relax, back they go.

Let this easy, natural breath return to you as a body habit. Through the stress of life we shorten our breath. What a huge mistake that is. Take the time to let yourself return to access this essential birthright—an easy, full breath.

Step Two

The next step can be done alone or combined with a warm-up or two covered in chapter 10. In this you use your natural breath, drawing it into the lungs, and at the same time imagine you are calling chi into your body directly—through the air, through the skin, and into the tan t'ien. Actually focus on the tan t'ien as you breathe. This single exercise has days of potential experience in it, simple to do and vastly useful as you move through the day.

Step Three

The third step in this sequence is to draw the breath through the nose into the lungs and imagine you are drawing the chi not only through air coming into your nose, but directly into the tan t'ien. It can feel as if you are drawing it down from the lungs, or in from in front of the tan t'ien, or from all the air surrounding the pelvis, or all the chi surrounding the entire body. It doesn't matter how you envision it. Just imagine bringing chi straight to the tan t'ien, however it is best for you to imagine it. Relax on the exhale and inhale air and chi again. In this way you have two breaths: the breath of air and the breath of chi. As you do the exercise, the oxygen and chi both disperse without further mutual guidance. All you do is breathe and feel your lungs and pelvis energize.

A handy new device is now available called breath strips. They are strips of sticky plastic that you put over the bridge of the nose and attach to the sides of the nostrils. The tension of the strip flares the nostrils just slightly, and viola—breath is easier. Often when we have reached our mature years we also have some obstruction to breathing, particularly when asleep. This strip addresses the problem of having less oxygen and chi available. Who knows, maybe some brain aging is due to this common problem—oxygen and chi deprivation while sleeping. Grab those strips!

Breathing into the Governing Vessel

Guide the chi into a specific energetic meridian in the body called the governing vessel. This is the central meridian, a coursing energetic flow that circles the body front to back, from head to perineum. It is a bit trickier to do this if you require concrete feedback, so let your subjective experience dominate. When you breathe chi into the tan t'ien, you usually feel warmth and pelvic aliveness. That is success. The chi obeys your envisioning commands, even if you can't feel much. Give yourself time, and it will become clearer. Eventually you will feel the meridian become lively.

To begin, breathe normally. Breathe into the lungs, relax, and let it flow out. The central meridian flow rises from the perineum up the center of the front and back of the body. The flows meet at the lips. The belief is that this flow was a steady, circular current in utero and upon birth it became essentially two flows drawing from the same source—the perineum.

Bring your focus to your chi. Breathe through the pores. Synchronistically with your breathing, your chi descends into your tan t'ien. Now demand that the chi drop into your perineum as you continue to inhale air. Breathing naturally, let the chi rise up your spine and down to the upper lip. At the same time, exhale your air breath through your nose, up the front and center of your torso, and to the lower lip. They meet and merge. Your focus stays on your tan' t'ien and the flow up the spine and up the front of your torso to your lips. This breath exercise energizes and relaxes simultaneously—a nice combination.

Heavy Low/Lighten Up

Balanced energy is a key to a life of longevity. The role the tan t'ien plays in maintaining balance is key, even critical. If your breath is not united with the all-important tan t'ien, your upper body becomes heavier feeling than your lower body. When the upper body is heavier than the lower, it throws off many internal systems, but one of the most obvious is that it becomes all too easy to misstep. But when uniting breath with the tan t'ien, the reverse happens.

Try it. Direct your chi, on the breath, into the tan t'ien. The lower part of your body feels heavier and the upper body feels lighter and balance improves.

This is one of the basics of T'ai Chi—you heavy-up the lower, below the waist, and you let the upper, above the waist, become lighter and lighter.

When you're heavy in the top—or not directing chi to the tan t'ien—you lose your center of gravity. This throws off the natural movement of your body and produces undue tension and stress in all the simple and frequent acts of movement. The stress and tension build-up in the muscle is not easily relieved. This muscle holding accounts for many nights of poor sleep and days of not feeling deeply rested. Just the simple task of remembering throughout the day to direct chi to the tan t'ien will help this problem. The center of gravity strengthens fast when you put your developed attention to your tan t'ien and right away your held muscles can relax. No longer needing to hold up unnecessarily, they let go. Below the waist becomes the foundation and the upper body is free to move with ease. This natural occurrence in the body is simple because there is finally enough oxygen and chi to run the mechanism of your body well. The body relaxes and a feeling of deep refreshment fills you.

Now when you practice these techniques in your life you will be well equipped to follow the T'ai Chi instructor of your choice as he or she advises you to let the lower get heavy and let the upper become light. You will already know how to direct your breath to accomplish this. Your learning curve in getting the actual movements will evolve more smoothly.

More Breathing Exercises

If you like these breath exercises, you might enjoy a few more. Each different breath style fills a practical function. The previous ones increased chi, redistributed the center of gravity, and vitalized the all-important governing vessel, for improved liveliness, coordination, and balance.

Reverse Breath (T'ai Chi Pre-birth Breath)

The Reverse Breath technique is also known as the Pre-birth Breath. This name comes from the belief that this breath technique imitates the natural breath of the fetus. As a fetus, we are filled with the most youthful and rejuvenating chi. The function of this chi is to build a new body. Pre-birth chi was valued as the key to reversing and slowing down the aging process.

Nourishment, oxygen, and chi are drawn into the fetus through the umbilical cord, and each courses through the body, with chi heading straight into the tan t'ien. Then it is dispersed throughout the little growing body to nourish its life. Because the umbilical cord's connecting point is in the abdomen, the fetus is seen as drawing its life-giving fuels into the lower abdomen, rather than the lungs. The fetus is seen as drawing these fuels into the body by expanding the abdomen to receive them. Then it does the reverse: tightens the abdomen to rid itself of toxins. ("Normal" breath begins at the moment the child is separated from the mother by the severing of the umbilical cord.)

Are you breathing from the throat? Qi cultivates breathing from your tan t'ien.

If your breath is smooth, if your mind is calm, you have a clear wellspring of vitality.

The T'ai Chi Pre-birth Breath is designed to emulate this early state of development. It rejuvenates and builds the body by deliberately accessing pre-birth chi.

The masters believed only pre-birth chi could reverse the aging process. It's a wonderful claim and there is nothing to lose in trying. To do this breath, you are simply going to reverse the place you expand to receive the chi. Let's begin: Take a deep breath, and as you inhale through your nose, contract or pull your abdominal muscles in toward your spine and up into the ribcage. As you

> Many people practice T'ai Chi for the moving meditation quality. Simply through the act of focusing our attention on the matter at hand, the mind quiets naturally. In sports this is often called "being in the zone," and in T'ai Chi practice we cultivate the ability to settle into this state of mind at will. Proper execution of the form requires paying attention to small details of movement and allowing the energy (chi) and breath to move freely. These details are difficult, if not impossible, to execute correctly without a peaceful quality of mindfulness so we have a way of easily checking ourselves.
>
> As practitioners become more skillful at this, they find this quality appearing spontaneously in their daily lives. This is a benefit that moving meditation can provide that may be more difficult to obtain through sitting meditation practices. Perhaps this is because the state cultivated in T'ai Chi is one defined by acting skillfully in the world, with physical balance and control. The quiescent awareness gained through sitting meditation, on the other hand, may be more easily overwhelmed by the pressures of our daily responsibilities.
>
> —Fernando Raynolds

exhale through your mouth, you expand these out, rounding out the abdomen. Your attention on this reverse action will keep you from returning to the natural, or post-birth, breathing.

At this point the breathing exercise takes on another dimension—sound. Sound deepens the effectiveness of the rejuvenation and is another interesting aspect to incorporate. The power of breath and the power of sound were joined into the To Noa. Post-birth, or natural, breath has the sound "Haah." Haah is said as the inhale expands the abdomen and lifts the lungs. "Heng" is said as you exhale and the abdomen tightens back and up, and the lungs lower.

Allow your lower half to become heavy and stable. As you do this, your upper torso will become lighter and more relaxed. Now return to your breath. Let the words combine with the breath. Haah-inhale, pause, heng-exhale, pause, haah-inhale, pause, heng-exhale. . . . It is like a circle of breath and sound moving in and out. Both the nose and mouth are inhaling and exhaling. Let the rhythm or speed of your breath remain normal to discourage hyperventilation.

Now try it with your fingers loosely knit, hold them over your abdomen. As you contract your abdomen back and up, inhale and aloud say "heng." This action draws the precious pre-birth chi upward from the tan t'ien to the diaphragm. It is the chi's transition into the diaphragm that begins to make pre-birth chi available to your body. After the chi has transitioned from the tan t'ien into the diaphragm, do a short, sharp inhale through the nose. This directs the post-birth chi into the lungs. Hold your breath, and the pre-birth chi mingles with the post-birth chi. Coursing together throughout the meridians, they create the rejuvenating results. Say "haah" as you exhale, through the mouth. Upon the exhalation, the post-birth chi is exhaled to the surrounding chi field. The pre-birth chi returns to its home in the tan t'ien.

Develop a familiar, friendly relationship to this exercise and it will become a welcome ally. A few minutes a few times a day, in fresh air if possible, will provide a stable familiarity for you. From then on you will be able to access it easily. Once this solidifying has occurred, you are ready to move on to combining the words with your Pre-birth, or Reverse, Breath.

Adding Intent to the Reverse Breath

What have we accomplished so far? The breath has brought in the chi. The pre-birth chi has been lifted through the body. Now let's bring the chi in to penetrate every part of your body. This is achieved in a two-pronged effort—body movement and mental focus or intent. Your intent directs the movement of chi—it moves the chi into and throughout your body and connects your chi field to the outer field of chi that bonds all. Most people don't think consciously one little bit about moving chi. Lucky for them, a fair amount of chi intake is as automatic as air intake. What we are doing here is knocking it up a notch or two. By combining exercise—breath and movement—with sound and focused intent, you increase your capacity for liveliness, thanks to increased oxygen intake and improved chi.

To direct chi, imagine or visualize, as you prefer, your chi moving where you want it. Imagine it moving from inside to outside as you inhale and exhale. Imagine it sinking into that little storehouse of power, your tan t'ien. Imagine it moving to a joint, a finger, whatever. Wherever you see it going, there it will go. It follows your demand. Now combine your mental demand with movement. Inhale through your nose, chi rushes in. Organs lift as you raise your arms up to shoulder height. Chi rushes in from the outside to the inside and you can feel it contributing to the lifting of the arms. Your arms lift as if in water, and now stretch out, palms out, resting on the water. Exhale and arms relax to your side. This is actually very basic Qigong.

> When inhaling, your earth chi rises. When exhaling, your heaven chi descends. When you breathe into the tan t'ien, your Qi is the connection with heaven and earth Qi.

Ready for the next one? Place your feet shoulder-width apart, legs heavy and stable, arms light and relaxed at your side. Bring your attention to your tan t'ien. Without breathing, slowly raise the arms, palms facing downward, fingers are relaxed and pointing downward, limp wrists. Arms are reaching to the side at shoulder level and resting on water. Now inhale through your nose, soundlessly, and contract your abdomen in and up. Saying "haah," exhale orally, as you straighten your hands and fingers, up through the weight of the water, palms to earth. The abdomen expands out. Push out the breath. The pre-birth chi sinks again to the tan t'ien. Arms float down to the sides.

The appropriate places for these exercises abound: in preparation for T'ai Chi, prior to prayer or meditation, before a challenging conversation, or to stabilize our overly emotional inner world. In addition to its traditional application—rejuvenation—it is relaxing.

Practicing Breath Exercises

The major principles to be applied to breath exercises are:

1. Relax, don't make effort, don't make it into a big deal.
   Effortless is best.
2. Use your thought to direct your chi.
3. Standing or sitting, let your lower body, from the waist down, become as stable as a mountain.
4. As you breathe and move, cultivate the feeling of stability in your legs.
5. Don't be speedy or go too long.
6. Be as regular with your breath exercise as you are with your tooth care.

These beginning breath and T'ai Chi practices will establish a wonderful increase in your internal liveliness, power, and strength. When doing these exercises standing, clarity comes quickly about where your unnecessary tension is residing. These unnecessarily taught areas get achy, twitchy, and generally uncomfortable. Only releasing the tension relieves these annoyances, and away goes tension, down the drain.

A good technique for tension relief is to again use your mind to direct chi to the area. Breathe as if your breath is going into and being absorbed by the area of your choice. Now just allow the area to relax down. Even if it is a bone or joint that really doesn't relax, the command is useful for producing a more relaxed and efficient area.

When you find the time to access this inner world of chi relaxation, your body will be open, and chi as well as oxygen will circulate more effectively throughout. Generally, these exercises do not create problems if you normally

Breath had always been critical to Kate because she loved to smoke. She started young, loved it, and had no desire to quit despite the pleas from family and friends. She started Qigong because her daughter wanted to do it with her. They had a great time and loved the class. Then there was a very unexpected occurrence. Kate began to crave her precious ciggies less. Her body didn't remind her as often to pick one up. When she realized she was smoking from habit rather than craving, she decided to smoke only when she craved it. That was when she enjoyed the smoking ritual the most. Over time her craving for the cigarettes continued to decrease. She continued to smoke only when she really enjoyed it. What this evolved into was having a cigarette or two in the evening. She has never felt better and she has never enjoyed her smoking more.

have shortness of breath. In fact, as the T'ai Chi practice sessions accumulate, you will have an easier flow of breath. These exercises do not make excessive demands on the body. Oxygen debt is the result of muscles demanding more oxygen than can be received. T'ai Chi should never create this response. Your oxygen intake, chi absorption, and muscle demands will balance perfectly, leaving you refreshed, alert, and lively. If this turns out not to be true for you, talk to your teacher and your doctor. T'ai Chi is meant to be done with absolute respect for the benign pace, gentle breath, and the directing of chi. This encourages your body to greater health instead of you dragging your body along in a more strenuous exercise because it's "good for you," even though it may also cause injury. The very nature of T'ai Chi movements coupled with breath exercise is self-regulatory. The partnership of the two regulates oxygen consumption and the oxygen needs of the body, providing a perfect balance for health and an immediate feeling of being deeply refreshed.

For your own practice it might be useful to have a daily breathing checklist.

1. Have you allowed natural breath?
2. Are you relaxing your abdomen?
3. Are you relaxed enough to receive a slow, deep inhale?
4. Are you relaxed enough to let the breath flow out on its own?
5. Have you included Pre-birth Breath?
     • Rest your fingers lightly at the tan t'ien
     • Inhale and draw your abdomen in and up
     • Your exhale flows out and the abdomen rounds out

Chapter 8

Qigong Breath

The history of Qigong is even more obscure than that of T'ai Chi. Older than T'ai Chi Ch'uan, it is believed by some to date back to prehistoric humankind. Paintings unearthed in China date back at least 3,000 years and contain images of people doing an activity that appears to be Qigong. What is eminently clear through this obscure background is that Qigong is old and valued, and has been a basic, frequently-used, and passed-on tool for health for thousands of years. In fact, Qigong has such a long and sought after history that it really ceases to have a unique history of its own. Qigong became so deeply ingrained in the exercise habits of the East that its root of wisdom can be found in all the health disciplines coming from China and surrounding nations. Qigong provided the foundation for accessing chi in five disciplines seeking self-improvement and greater clarity: Buddhism, Taoism, Confucianism, martial arts, and health.

It is likely that T'ai Chi as we know it today was deeply impacted by the masterful breath exercise Qigong, which is also sometimes called Chi Kung. This discipline places emphasis on drawing in maximum vitality from the breath—filling up with it, storing some, and using the rest effectively. When we engage in deliberately circulating chi, we can quite realistically take charge of our inner force and vitality. As we can garner our inner vitality, our ability to take charge of our mental, physical, emotional, and spiritual well-being becomes increasingly available—this is the value of Qigong.

Learning Qigong along with T'ai Chi supports so many aspects of life: health, mind expansion, focus, spiritual cultivation, and faster reflexes. Qigong builds the inner, T'ai Chi builds the outer. Combining them, as is often done in T'ai Chi, is the very best of both worlds.

Some T'ai Chi teachers recommend learning Qigong prior to learning the sequential moves of T'ai Chi. The reason is simple: Qigong is a breath discipline that utilizes minor body movements. While these movements are essential, they are simple, and they have the added benefit of being easy to remember. The greatest challenge in T'ai Chi is usually just remembering the movements—what comes next, how is that foot supposed to go, where is my weight supposed to be now? So, as you wind your way through T'ai Chi, step-by-flowing-step, you can have a familiarity with Qigong well settled into your bones. The effects are marvelous, the breath control rejuvenating, and the movement is far from intimidating.

Understanding Qigong Breath

Initially, Qigong breath is presented in a way that is very similar to T'ai Chi's natural breath. Qigong is often described as emulating a child's breath, which is low in the abdomen. As young children, we are more present and more engaged in life. One reason for this is that we've had a fewer number of bad experiences. Over time, bad experiences build up and we develop a protective reaction to a life loaded with fear. When this reaction occurs the breath restricts, which leads to the limiting of our chi intake. Chi brings us not only health and well-being, but also presence. It takes very few years, and sometimes only a matter of a few really bad weeks, before we begin to deeply restrict our intake and exhale of breath. The deep and open breath we experience as a child will naturally constrict and tighten as we experience a series of misfortunes or accidents.

When breath is restricted and chi is reduced, we are not adequately preparing ourselves for the inevitable uncertainties of life. Actually, we become very poorly prepared. When a life event occurs—a near miss in a car, achy joints, problems in the family, disturbing national or international events—we move from stressed to more stressed, and the feeling of well-being can become an ancient memory. This stressed reaction is not good for promoting a sense of inner confidence and makes us more susceptible to constructing an unwise response that will compound the difficult situation and drive stress up further. A cycle is formed and too often never broken. We keep ourselves, through oxygen and chi deficit, in a limited state of well-being. Not even in sleep can the chi and oxygen debt be refilled.

The goal of Qigong then is to develop breath that, despite the vagaries of life, stays deep and full. Qigong provides the self-awareness and the tools to readjust breath if the shallow breathing begins to dominate again. By practicing Qigong on a

> Without internal force you cannot develop good health.
> —Wong Kiew Kit

> Make a habit of concentrating on the chi. This can be done at work or at play, walking or riding. Formation of the habit requires perseverance, but is infinitely better and far less expensive than the modern practice of regular ingestion of medicines.
> —Cheng Man-Ch'ing and Robert Smith

regular basis, the body, mind, and spirit learn how to work together for a better life perspective. The more Qigong fills you with chi, the more your ability to be fully in the pleasures of your life increases. It may be the same old life, but it won't look that way. However much you like your life now, you will enjoy it even more filled to the tippy-top with chi and oxygen.

Benefits of Qigong

For most of us, our bodies are doing very little as our minds race along. Sitting in cars, before computers, or being entertained can occupy seventy-five percent of the day. Qigong helps offset this downward spiral of high-energy mind and diminished body zeal by allowing the breath/chi/oxygen to penetrate the muscles, ligaments, and bones. Breath drops to the abdomen, chi begins to sink to tan t'ien, and the body breathes a sigh of relief. The breath banquet has started.

As you practice Qigong, your tan t'ien will become a most important storage vessel, one that will actually cultivate the chi as you continue doing Qigong. When the tan t'ien is full (and the frequent Qigong exercises encourage ongoing cultivation) the life force rises to be high and healthy. As your T'ai Chi practice complements your Qigong exercises, your chi becomes more balanced, more refined, and offers great spiritual awareness. This certainly is a major improvement over the frequently poor or declining health and lack of personal well-being so often witnessed in older years.

> Energy training in Qigong falls into two main categories: increasing the amount of vital energy in the body and promoting harmonious energy flow.
> —Wong Kiew Kit

As you attain the balance of chi, your moodiness will abate. Irritability, fear, anxiety, and even states of depression will weaken and then give way to that good old feeling of well-being. Though these negative feelings don't really disappear, they will recede to become a smaller part of your emotional life—no longer looming larger than the rest but there for access at the appropriate moment. Then instead of claiming too much of you, they are free to remerge into balanced emotion again as well-being returns more quickly and easily.

Emotions directly affect chi. For example, anger causes chi to become coarse and harsh. When this happens, your feet lose their ground and your personal sense of harmony is lost. You will find that practicing Qigong will return your chi to peaceful clarity. When your chi is peaceful and clear, harmony will reign in your inner world.

Remember your breath and fill yourself regularly. You will find that Qigong will increase your chi flow so you can focus and deliver as you choose. As you successfully root your chi into your body through Qigong, you can direct it as you choose: To energize yourself, focus on the tan t'ien. To clear up your thoughts, focus on the head and spine. To stabilize your body, breathe chi into

> The chi should be stimulated. After the stimulation of the chi, it becomes so hot that it penetrates into the bone and becomes marrow. The chi should sink to the tan t'ien (one and one-third inches below the navel). When your chi sinks to the tan t'ien, the whole body will be relaxed and the blood will circulate freely throughout the body. When you practice the T'ai Chi postures in this manner for a long period of time, you will enjoy perfect health.
>
> —Master T. T. Liang

your legs and hips for heaviness. To relax yourself, fill everywhere with chi and then let it drain out of your tense areas like sand. To settle your nerves, breathe chi into the tan t'ien. These are but a few ways Qigong can improve your comfort by purposely directing chi to a problem area. Inner calm, force, and vitality—the ageless triune.

There are eight basic Qigong breath practices.

Breathing Principles of Qigong Breath

1. *Natural Breathing.* The regular breath one takes constantly without awareness.
2. *Cleansing Breath.* Inhaling through the nose and exhaling through the mouth.
3. *Tonic Breath.* Inhaling through the mouth and exhaling through the nose.
4. *Alternate Breath.* Inhale through one nostril, exhale through the other.
5. *Natural Deep Breath.* That natural deep breath taken spontaneously.
6. *Long Breath.* Abdominal breathing.
7. *Reverse Long Breath.* Abdomen expands when exhaling and contracts when inhaling
8. *Tortoise Breath.* Mastery breathing. This is a type of very slow breathing that occurs naturally in masters, often after decades of daily practice.

You will probably be surprised at how easily you learn the skill of Qigong. The movements consist of bending and straightening in the legs, an occasional repositioning of the legs and arm motions that are large and comfortable. This is then done with the breath. Take the time to learn this and you will be able to do the full form in a regular routine or slip in just a bit at a time when you need a break. It will give you a mini inner vacation. A de-stressor at your fingertips!

After you have gotten past the time when the practice takes place with the instruction, then you can do it anywhere. In fresh air, under the blue sky, greeting the day with the dew under your feet is the ancient ideal. If this works for you, great. If not, do it as you find best for you.

You will need:

- Your best shot at clean air
- Space to move
- Comfortable, roomy clothes

That's it.

Qigong will support you where you are, right now. You don't need to change a thing. Wherever you are, whoever you are, whatever shape you have or are in, just start. It will be right there for you, sick or well. Your need to drop back on exercise when you don't feel well won't apply here. You can do Qigong sick and you can do Qigong well. You can do it hiking the Pacific Crest Trail or lying in a hospital bed with only a toe to wiggle. It stands on its own, joins you wherever you are, and also paves the way for T'ai Chi. Learn it, and it will always be there for you. What could be more natural?

It is hard for me to believe, but I am now over seventy. I sometimes have trouble with getting cold, then I have a devil of a time warming up. Practicing Qigong has helped me with this "senior" problem. I think this is a result of my improved circulation into my arms and legs. I also learned a neat Qigong trick. If I get cold, I rub my ears very gently for a few minutes. I warm right up. My memory has improved too! Not as many senior moments.

—Helen, a 5-year Qigong/T'ai Chi student

Chapter 9

Qigong Practice

A Qigong student studied with a master in China some years ago. The master was well known. A chi healing center had been erected for him to teach Qigong for specific health concerns. No one was turned away. The belief was that where there is breath, there is life, and where there is life, there is the ability to renew. Since no one was turned away, many were confined to sitting or lying in beds. It made no difference. The Qigong practices went on as usual. The only difference between those who could move easily and those who could not was the range of movement. But there was no difference at all in the ability to direct chi. They just moved whatever they could, even if it was just one toe. In some cases the bedridden were better at it because their minds focused on their bodies more easily. Rates of renewal varied, but over time people found better health and as a result a more satisfying well-being. The breath was very useful for creating better circulation, but the essential component was the ability to direct chi as the body needed it.

Each Qigong format carries this as its essential quality, to breathe, to follow the sequences, and most especially direct the chi in harmony with the potential that breath opens. Make Qigong your own. Learn the sequence so you are able to go from start to finish in one flowing motion. Breath, motion, and mind combine. You will find, like the people at the health center in China, that Qigong returns liveliness to your body and mind.

After you learn the sequences presented in this chapter, they are best done in an unbroken, flowing sequence without pause and with breath and movement combined as one. These movements are easy to learn and are remarkably effective—there is no chance for mistakes. And if you are T'ai Chi bound, they will prepare your internal body for T'ai Chi.

There are a few salient points to remember:

- *Relax*
  Let your entire body sink downwards. Let your shoulders relax, and keep your head suspended so that your spine stretches and relaxes. Make your lower body solid, stable like a mountain. If you aren't standing, still form these perceptions in your mind and transmit them to your body as best you can. Relax into this solid base that sits so securely from the waist down. As your lower half heavies up, feel your upper body become lighter and lighter.
- *Float through the Whole Thing*
  This is a non-forcing, gentle, flow of arm and hand movements. Move as if you are in water from the neck to the feet. Move within the gentle resistance. These are excellent exercises for anyone who needs to sit or lie down since the feet never move and the knees bend only slightly a few times.
- *Never Lock the Joints*
  Practice standing and straightening your arm and fingers without locking the joints. Chi either flows through the joints or it doesn't, in which case pain and inflammation result. If a joint is locked, it stalls the naturally flowing chi. If the chi is stalled or backlogged at the joints, it isn't free to move through the muscles and meridians of the body. Practice standing with the knees unlocked. Practice extending the arm with the shoulders

---

Breathing: Reverse Breathing

Many T'ai Chi and Qigong instructors differentiate between what is called prenatal and postnatal breathing. On the face of it, this can be confusing since clearly we don't breathe while in the womb.

Postnatal, or Buddhist, breathing is what humans naturally do when at rest. As the diaphragm drops with the inhale, the abdomen goes out, then the chest fills, and with a deep breath, the rib cage rises. As the ribs rise, they move up from the pelvis, drawing the abdomen in a bit. On the exhale, the lungs empty and the supporting musculature relaxes.

Prenatal breathing is also called Reverse or Taoist breathing. The prenatal name makes sense when you consider how you breathe when you are in a fetal position. As we inhale, the expansion of the chest cavity occurs in the area of greatest freedom. In the fetal position, expansion in the front of the body is restricted, so the expansion naturally occurs in the back and sides. Breathing in this fashion creates gentle movement in the spine which may not occur during a normal breath, and this, in turn, facilitates the flow of chi.

Reverse breathing occurs naturally whenever the expansion of the front of the body is restricted. For instance, when we push something—say a truck out of a ditch—in order to push strongly, the abdomen must be firmed and the chest is constricted by the use of the arms. Consequently, the expansion of the inhale occurs primarily in the back and along the sides of the abdomen. In T'ai Chi practice, if the form is done correctly, with isometric tone between the legs, the abdomen will be somewhat firmed and the breath will naturally flow in the prenatal fashion.

—Fernando Raynolds

down and the elbows unlocked. Practice extending the fingers without locking the joints.

- *Practice Daily*
  This is essential for progress with your Qigong. Like many, many disciplines, the more you do it, the deeper it goes and the more you get from it. When you see someone doing it, it may appear that they are doing the same old thing over and over again. But to the person actually doing Qigong it is different every day. As the body, breath, and chi open, the inner life of health burgeons and the spirit lifts. As the movements become easier and easier to remember, their influence will be more and more compelling.

The Sequence

There are many, many forms of Qigong, especially since it has now started to become almost as popular as T'ai Chi. Some movements more elaborate, others far simpler. The following Qigong series is an adaptation of a Qigong series from the wonderful book *The Tao of T'ai Chi Ch'uan, Way to Rejuvenation* by master Jwa, Tsung Hwa. Avail yourself of the advice about breath control by finding a copy (there is information about it in the resources section of this book).

This entire series can be done sitting or lying down. Simply adapt the movements while maintaining the breath and abdomen expansions and contractions. Do the movements to the best of your ability. Follow every instruction you are able to manage. You will find that with a little flexibility, this series of Qigong adapts quite nicely. Then if you move only your toe, you can still imagine or visualize yourself doing the entire sequence. You might accomplish this best with your eyes closed. Your energy body is intact. The chi flows will move throughout, whether your muscles move well or not. It is this chi flow, nurtured by your breath and directed by your mind, that we are reaching for here. Enjoy, be diligent, and let your chi begin to bring you some renewal of body, mind, and spirit.

Now let's begin. Eyes soft and gently focused.

POSITION 1

Standing (or sitting or lying, if needed).

Feet shoulder width apart.

Knees straight and soft.

Arms relaxed at your sides.

Relax into your body, your head light as an imaginary string gently lifts it upward, extending and straightening the spine.

Breathe naturally and easily to the tan t'ien, and let your body prepare for the increase in breath and chi.

POSITION 2A

Float your arms up at the side to shoulder height and relax them to be supported as if on water.

Your palms are facing downward to earth and your wrists are relaxed and limp. Your fingers point down.

Inhale through your nose, contracting your abdomen as you move your arms upward.

POSITION 2B

Exhale through your mouth, expanding your abdomen.

As you exhale, straighten your hands, initiating movement at your wrists while your arms float submerged in the water. Your wrists bring your fingers up.

Straighten your fingers, palms directed down toward earth, shoulders relaxed.

Tip: A good way to keep your shoulders relaxed is to feel your shoulder blade muscle pulling down as you extend your arms up and down.

POSITION 3A
Contract your abdomen.
Float your arms to extend to the front of
your body.
Your right wrist crosses over your left,
your palms face down to earth.
Your fingers are relaxed though extended.
Inhale, keeping your abdomen contracted.

POSITION 3B
With your arms floating and your
shoulders relaxed downward, relax your
wrists and allow your palms to float
down to face your body.
Exhale from your mouth.

POSITION 4A (RIGHT)
Contract your lower abdomen and direct
    your hands in toward your body, keeping
    your wrists crossed.
Your head elevates upward, extending the
    spine.
Breathe naturally.

POSITION 4B (BELOW, LEFT)
Unfold your arms and float them to the
    sides, palms forward.
Simultaneously and gradually straighten
    your knees.
Inhale and contract your abdomen.

POSITION 4C (BELOW, RIGHT)
Float your palms up toward heaven, and
    now out.
Bring your arms to the front of your body.
Exhale through the mouth.
Your abdomen expands.

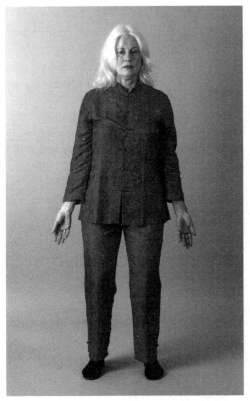

POSITION 5A
Contract your abdomen.
Inhale through the nose
as you float your arms
to your sides, shoulder
height.
Your palms are toward
heaven.
Your fingers are relaxed
and your legs are
straight, knees soft.

POSITION 5B
Exhale through your
mouth and expand your
abdomen.
As you exhale, straighten
your arms, open your
hands, and extend your
fingers. Stretch your
hands and fingers.
Relax on the water.

POSITION 6A
Contract your abdomen.
Your head lifts upward, extending the spine.
Inhale through your nose, with your abdomen still contracted. Make a loose fist with your hands and bend your elbows, bringing your fists to face your ears.
Gradually turn your fists to face outward.

POSITION 6B
Exhale through your mouth and extend your abdomen.
Simultaneously straighten out your legs and float your arms to shoulder level.
Gently open your fists, relax your palms, and extend your fingers.
Your palms face downward.

POSITION 7A (TOP AND BOTTOM)
Contract your abdomen.
Repeat the previous Position 6 with one change: As you inhale, abdomen contracted, you bend your elbows, bring your fists to your ears, then extend your arms upward over your head, straight but not locked.

POSITION 7B (LEFT)
Opening your fists, extend upward on your legs, stand up on your tiptoes (or, if sitting or in bed, point your toes and think of standing on them), extend your arms and raise your hands over your head.
Cross your hands, right palm in back of left hand, with palms facing front, and exhale through your mouth, abdomen extended.

POSITIONS 8A AND 8B

Remain on your toes and gradually lower
your arms in a circular fashion so they
naturally float together, with your hands
meeting at the tan t'ien.

Your hands grasp each other, with the
right palm over the back of the left
hand, thumbs touch each other.

As this movement occurs, inhale through
your nose, abdomen expands.

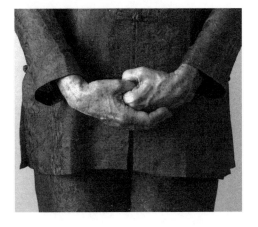

POSITION 8C

Lowering your body so your feet are flat
on the ground, exhale from your
mouth, as your abdomen expands.

The hands stay laced at the tan t'ien.

POSITION 9A

Hold your entire body straight and still.

Lift your head upward, extending your spine.

Moving only your head, turn and look over your left shoulder (hands are still laced at the tan t'ien), inhale and contract your abdomen.

POSITION 9B

Exhale, extend your abdomen, turn your head only as your body rests in steady stillness. Look to the front, eyes soft and slightly unfocused.

Repeat the sequences of Positions 9A and 9B on alternate sides. Keep the breath technique exactly the same.

Repeat three to five times. End on the right side.

POSITION 10A
Contract your abdomen and then inhale
  through your nose as you simultaneously
  lift your joined hands to your chest.
Your palms face toward you.

POSITION 10B
Exhale through your mouth.
Extend your abdomen.
Turn your palms face down and float them
  to the floor as you bend from the waist.
Positions 10A and 10B should be repeated
  from three to five times in sequence.
As you move to repeat the sequence,
  inhale and become erect by rolling your
  spine up and as if a sprout is growing
  up from the base of your spine.
Imagine that the sprout, not your muscles,
  is bringing you erect.

POSITION 11A

Contract your abdomen and inhale through your nose while rising from the floor.

When erect, cross your wrists in front of your chest, right over left, with your palms facing your body.

POSITION 11B

Exhale through the mouth, expand your abdomen, lift your left palm flat to the sky, and press your right palm down, flat to the earth.

Repeat sequence of Positions 11A and 11B three to five times by returning the crossed hand to your heart center and alternating your extending arms. The first sequence is right to heaven, left to earth, and left wrist is over right. End when your right palm is to sky.

POSITION 12A
Contract your abdomen, inhale through your nose. Simultaneously with the inhale, lower your right arm as you raise your left arm until they are both evenly extended at your sides. They are shoulder height, palms down.
Wrists are relaxed and limp.

POSITION 12B
Exhale through your mouth and extend your abdomen.
Float your arms on water as you extend your hands and fingers, with your palms facing toward earth.

POSITION 13A
Contract your abdomen as you inhale through your nose.
Float your arms toward the front of your body.
Place your right wrist over your left, with your palms facing down toward earth.

POSITION 13B
Exhale through your mouth and expand your abdomen, allowing your wrists to relax, and float the hand downward, palms toward your body, fingers relaxed.

POSITION 14A

Contract your abdomen and inhale
through your nose as you lower your
hands, turning them toward the body.
When your arms have naturally floated
down, they release in front of your
thighs.

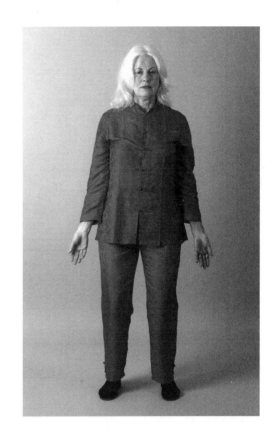

POSITION 14B

Return your left palm to lay on your right
palm, with your thumbs touching each
other.
Straighten your legs and bring joined hand
up to your tan t'ien.

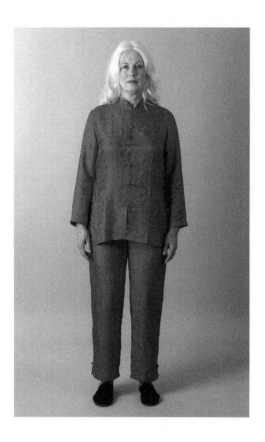

POSITION 14C
Exhale through your mouth and expand
    your abdomen.
Turn your joined palms down to earth and
    let them separate as your arms gently
    float to your sides.
Rest within the form of your body.
Breathe and relax, relax, relax.
Wait a few minutes before moving on into
    your next event.

This completes a wonderful traditional Qigong. You will become more familiar with the movements and how to coordinate your breath and abdominal movements as you practice. This familiarity will bring you a newfound sense of the movements actually emanating from the tan t'ien. As the chi movement strengthens in your body, the chi joins with the muscle action. This is directed by your mind as you go through remembering and refining the sequences. It is this distillation of chi, blood, and muscle that facilitates the floating concept until you feel as if you really are floating. The body, now filled with chi, becomes lighter and lighter. This occurs because the muscles are releasing their long-held stress and they work together in natural harmony. Thus, when filled with abundant chi, it does seem as if one can float the upper body on water while the lower body is stable and firm. This is the ideal state for our bodies, according to Chinese tradition, and this is emphasized in both Qigong and T'ai Chi.

Each time you practice this Qigong sequence, you will be a step closer to feeling this personally for yourself. Just keep on practicing!

Part Four

Practicing T'ai Chi

Chapter 10

Warm-ups:
Easy Steps to T'ai Chi

Are you ready to give this a try?
T'ai Chi will not hurt you in any way. Unlike yoga, running, or even walking, where some injury can occur, not so with this simple, flowing form, and it can be practiced in a twenty-minute commitment each day. So step in and see, one step at a time, what it has to offer you.

There are two ways to approach warm-ups. One is to do them in the "classic" style, in which you set aside an appropriate amount of time to do a certain sequence of demonstrated warm-ups prior to a T'ai Chi practice session. These warm-ups prepare the body for the stretches and bends and turns that you'll be doing in your T'ai Chi session. The second mode of warm-ups is to take a certain aspect of T'ai Chi movement and practice them whenever you feel is appropriate during your day, let's call this the "casual" style. Both styles of warm-ups are great for learning the T'ai Chi sequences, and they deliver gifts of vitality in their own right.

Both modes of warm-ups will be covered in this chapter. Let's look at the casual style first. In many ways this style of warm-up offers more gifts because it teaches you to integrate T'ai Chi into your everyday life—allowing you to bring enhanced ways of moving into your most personal actions. Where better for their ancient wisdom to assist you? Doing these warm-ups in a dedicated time and space allows the nervous system to be stimulated and also establishes familiarity. A perfect blend!

The only really hard part of T'ai Chi is first finding the time to do it, and second, not giving up too early because it is different and a bit of a stretch remembering the sequences. What you can use this book for is building your foundation, a foundation of understanding that will give you the information and confidence to move forward, when your time is right, with personal T'ai Chi instruction in a class situation, or with a private instructor. What we are

> To get the full value of joy, you must have somebody to share it with.
> —Mark Twain

> In any action the body should be light and agile. T'ai Chi will contribute to a light and agile body.

doing now is a method of instilling various aspects of T'ai Chi into your life, one aspect at a time. This incorporates the basic concepts into your daily life and rhythms naturally. In this way T'ai Chi won't be something you do just in the class and at home practice, but will much more easily infuse your everyday life with the ease and grace T'ai Chi offers you.

T'ai Chi teachers often talk about stepping into form as if you are stepping into a river—joining a moving flow already established and moving with or without you, a flow that you enter, move with, and then exit when practice is complete. These terminologies—entering the form, or having your teacher transmit the form to you, instead of teach—are part of T'ai Chi's ancient roots. Master taught student one to one in the structured Chinese culture of form and function. Becoming embodied, a kinesthetic description of coming into the form was an apt description of how it felt, and feels, to move into this ancient flow of movement, to become one more to embody it. Nowadays, when you see a group doing T'ai Chi together there is a cohesive quality in the form that each participant is contributing to with each movement.

The term "transmit the learning" also harkens back to ancient days of teaching. When the master and student had a total focus on the form and its execution, much time was taken with the student watching the master and over time mimicking his movements. There are those who feel that the greatest T'ai Chi masters never spoke to the student. The learning was done by: watch, practice, do. In this way only the finest students could achieve excellence. This is useful information for your own journey into developing greater T'ai Chi skills because it explains and supports the silence in which T'ai Chi is learned, practiced, and taught. It explains and supports the inner quiet world of the emphasis on the internal form, the action suited to one's own skill level, the embracing of T'ai Chi as a deeply personal experience and, most importantly, an experience that opens to you as you invite it in. And then within the joining of you and your fledgling T'ai Chi a deeper understanding occurs. This movement does have a form and a flow that accepts you at any level and gives you many gifts along the way. The transmitting of the form is a very personal experience. It is an experience that you cannot attain if you are criticizing yourself, trying to get it, attempting to rush yourself, or denying yourself the time in which you can find a satisfying union with T'ai Chi.

It is true there are many levels of expertise, many nuances of subtle movement. But from the early level on, and maybe always for you, T'ai Chi brings tools for more freedom in your body and health, and that is enough. Do the exercises as you can. Learn the form as you can. Enjoy the lovely and light ideas for learning the basics of T'ai Chi movement we are exploring here in this chapter. Let your learning of T'ai Chi be right where it is. And then enjoy it, as it is meant to bring pleasure and satisfaction.

The instructions or transmissions of T'ai Chi are meant to lead one into a greater state of inner peace and quiet focus. Any instruction you follow in this book is a guidepost to promoting both outer fluidity in your body structure and inner balance in your internal world. Something as simple as the Suspended String is an initial guide to both of these pleasurable outcomes. So if you do make the decision to suspend yourself each time your thoughts gently return to your commitment for the day—suspending from the string—you are starting to incorporate and learn the transmitting of T'ai Chi and you are also taking your first step into the form.

> Should you try T'ai Chi? If you take it seriously, you almost certainly will benefit. Older people may well find that arthritis pain is reduced and cardiovascular fitness improved. It helps reduce stress for many of all ages. It can increase muscle strength and balance generally, and improve overall functional status.
> —Barrie Cassileth, Chief of Integrative Medicine, Sloan-Kettering Cancer Center

There are a couple of ways to incorporate this initial transmission into your life. One is to do it as you think of it throughout the day. The other is to schedule in a period of time, say three minutes, where you keep this in mind for a length of time you have committed to. Then go on about your business, to return to another assigned time zone later in the day and evening. Whichever you choose, you will find over time that reminding yourself will become easier. You will find you are starting to do it without reminding yourself, that your body muscle memory is kicking in and this new posture of lengthening is becoming a much more natural addition to your life, even perhaps a natural everyday way of walking and moving. Self-reminding diminishes, and instead, this enhanced way of moving becomes natural. If T'ai Chi is anything, it is a proven route to natural health and well-being.

Casual Warm-ups

The casual style warm-ups, which we will discuss over the next few pages, are as follows:

- Suspended String
- Beach Walk
- Rock and Roll
- From the Hip
- Nature Walk
- Sprouting
- Stress to Sand

Suspended String

Right now, as you sit here reading, imagine that a string is attached to the crown of your head. With your head suspended from the string, feel your head gently lift your upper body more erect—just a bit. When you feel the head, and perhaps the spine, drawn easily up by thread at your crown, and your shoulders relax down, you are upright, and the shoulders are now more relaxed within the frame and structure of your body. This is your first step in T'ai Chi relaxation. No matter how erect or not really erect you are, this warm-up will help you to relax your shoulders, T'ai Chi style, within your structure.

> Your body's ability for maintaining health and overcoming illness is among nature's most remarkable feats. Your body is designed to heal itself. But you've been placed in a world that systematically interferes with this natural capacity, and your conscious involvement in your health is required if you are to truly prosper.
> —Donna Eden
> From "An Energy Sensitive Looks at Energy Psychology," keynote address at The First European Energy Psychology Conference, Lake Lucerne, Switzerland, July 3, 2001.

As you practice this warm-up, imagine you feel your torso becoming lighter and your legs and hips getting heavier, root. You are now more in tune with your tan t'ien. It is from here that you will eventually develop an initiating movement as you do your T'ai Chi. You will have the experience of the entire upper body relaxing down toward the tan t'ien and eventually more and more of your movements will emanate from this area.

Now, let the string pull up a bit. Now your neck length has increased a bit. Your head is feeling perhaps balanced on the occipital (the back part of your head). Gently turn your head from side to side. If the inner image of the string is strong, you might feel as if you are guiding the movement of your head as it hangs suspended from your thread. You may feel a bit freer and lighter. One suggestion would be to take this aspect of learning one of the cornerstones of T'ai Chi movement into your own movements for a full day. As you decide to let this warm-up become a part of your every day, you will be able to return to it again and again. As you sit, as you walk, as you watch TV, ride a bike, cook, feed the animals, read a story to a child, work on your hobby. . . all these natural occurrences in the day provide a perfect format for beginning T'ai Chi. Remember, T'ai Chi comes to meet you wherever you are, just open the door of your life.

Remembering several pointers will help you to incorporate this warm-up into your daily routines:

1. Don't get upset when you forget. Just return gently to your Suspended String.

2. If you feel achy in your muscles from this, that is fine. If you feel achy in your bones, then lift yourself a little less.

3. These are life enhancing additions. Enjoy your lightening and lengthening.

Beach Walk

After you have given time to sitting, walking, moving, and just generally living your life a little more elongated from the string, it will be time to take the next step, and this process does indeed have to do with stepping.

Do you have a memory of walking on sand? Imagine you are putting your feet, first one and then the other, down on sand, shifting your feet slightly as one does in sand to get a firmer footing. The sand comes up to your feet, forming against them, and as you release the full weight of your body, you'll be comfortably molded into the sand.

Why the sand fantasy? When placing your feet in T'ai Chi each step is taken with great sensitivity to the sole of the foot, its contact with the floor and also, very importantly, how much weight is on first one foot and then the other. To place your feet in sand on the floor where you are sitting, one at a time and both together, helps you develop the type of sensitivity to your feet that will greatly assist to your balance and your T'ai Chi form when you begin your learning.

Now try this sitting—wiggle your toes a bit and move your feet into contact with the floor's surface. Still sitting, with very small motions, shift your weight more to the heels, then rock slowly forward to have more weight on the balls of your feet. Come back to the weight being centered on each foot. Are your feet receiving even weight distribution, i.e., are both legs equally heavy on your foot? Now rock your feet, in a slow and subtle movement to the outside, and now roll just a bit onto the inside. Settle them back into the imagined sand. Your toes lightly resting on the "sand," the balls and heels of your feet settling into it.

Attending T'ai Chi classes twice a week may have significant health benefits for sedentary adults. Research published in the *American Journal of Preventive Medicine* reports that adults over age sixty-five who exercise the least have the most to gain from this Chinese exercise. Those with the most physical limitations reported the greatest improvement after six months of regular classes.

As we get older and then become elderly, the desire to retain independence is very high. But independence is dependant on one's ability to maintain self-care and cognitive functioning. It is important to launch into a personal care program that facilitates both of these requirements. Fortunately, T'ai Chi has been shown to improve and stabilize coordination and balance and to support healthy cognitive functioning. It is never too early or too late to start.

> Energies from the sun and the earth permeate every cell of your body, and they combine to form your energy body. Your energy body, in turn, is a distinct, self-regulating universe, a force that wells from within and radiates into the environment. It is continually interacting with the energies around it and moving its own energies to warm you, cool you, activate you, calm you, and establish a cycle of repair and rejuvenation. In this exquisite alchemy, energies are built up, stored, spent, transformed, harmonized, and brought into balance.
> —Donna Eden
> From "An Energy Sensitive Look at Energy Psychology,"
> keynote address at The First European Energy Psychology
> Conference, Lake Lucerne, Switzerland, July 3, 2001.

If your balance is not what you would like, this is an excellent exercise for beginning to become more surefooted. This is an easy sequence when you are sitting anywhere. It will begin to open the feet, ankles, and calves for the gentle shifting around back and forth that hallmarks T'ai Chi movements. This sequence of foot warm-ups is also easy to do standing. Actually, this is very effective in preparing for T'ai Chi. And you get so good at it that you will start to learn how to make the shift subtle so you aren't swaying in front of your friends like a palm in the wind. You can actually stand, string ascending, and very gently nestle your feet into "sand" as you wait in a line, as you wait for a live person on a voicemail number, when you are trying to catch your breath, as a friend repeats himself for the third time, or just when you plain old feel like it.

Depending on your zeal and ability, you can rest here with these two warm-ups or proceed to another. A word of advice: If you haven't gotten comfortable with the first two warm-ups as a part of your active life, then hold fast for a while until these seem very familiar and you are easy with them. No longer new and hard to remember, they are now comfortable and familiar.

If you have reached that point of familiar comfort, then let's go on.

Rock and Roll

This is a rotating movement that starts at the Suspended String and moves on down to the sand-nestled feet.

Standing as is, get some steadying support if you feel it wise, and feel the string lifting you up. (This can also be done sitting down.) Begin to rotate your head back and forth—not far and not fast—then from side to side. (You may hear crunching in your neck.) Your head is rotating from side to side suspended by the string. And you can feel the movement going down the neck and between your shoulders blades. Let your shoulders relax within your form as you continue to rotate.

Arms relaxed at your side, let the movement come down your spine into your hips. Easily and gently let your arms relax off of your relaxed shoulders, the rotating moves into the hips and as the hips rock side to side you can imagine the entire motion is actually being generated from there. The string continues to lengthen you, and your rotation is now generated at the hips. It actually may feel more solid to have this motion coming from your hip as the weight shifts a bit down your legs on to your feet still nestled in the "sand." As you get the nuance of the light movement generated at the hips, let your torso empty out— let all the weight in your torso sink to your hips and legs.

Remember, you are not attaining any goal, you're not trying to win any contest or to be the best or to be better than you are doing exactly as you do this. You are letting your hips move the rest of your body, rotating from side to side, as your head is stabilized by the string and your feet are secure in the sand. Actually, your entire body can become pretty relaxed within the rotation form. Your spine is responding to the lengthening and your feet are comfortably adjusting and readjusting to this swinging and you are swinging exactly the way you are comfortable. Let your knees relax a bit and it will make the swinging feel more graceful. Don't get dizzy or weird feeling. Find the movement, generated from your hips, that is just fine for you.

Clearly this complete action can't be integrated into your life as simply as the other two, so it requires a few minutes of time dedicated to it each day to get it. But what you can add in, pretty easily, is the fun of initiating movement from your hips.

From the Hip

Begin this warm-up not walking, but turning your torso from one side to another. Pretend you're standing in the kitchen and you are going to reach for a cup on the shelf. Usually one reaches with the hand and the arm leading, bringing the torso and finally the hips along behind it. Try it exactly opposite. Let your hips lead the movement, uniting with the spine coming into a twist, now the elbow rises from a relaxed shoulder, leading up to a relaxed, even limp hand. Your hand rises last, reaches for and grasps the glass, and then the hips once again lead the movement as the spine straightens and the elbow, not the shoulder, guides the hand to the counter surface. Remember how T'ai Chi often looks as if it is being done underwater. Try this, reaching as if through the gentle resistance of warm water from the neck down.

FROM THE HIP: STEP ONE

FROM THE HIP: STEP TWO   FROM THE HIP: STEP THREE

This movement, coming from the hips and bringing in the other parts of your body in graceful, relaxed attendance, is the core of T'ai Chi. The emphasis on the hips as the generator of movement is important for a very great reason: it activates the tan t'ien—which is dead center in the pelvis. And since chi is constantly being accumulated, gathered, and dispersed, it becomes critical to have an activity that brings constant, steady state of movement to the pelvis and that the movement be effectively coordinated with the chi-filled breath. T'ai Chi became the honed tool for this concert to occur.

This is the reason that T'ai Chi movement is always initiated from the pelvis. In this way your storehouse of chi in the tan t'ien is opened, nourished, and dispersed into the muscles and organs as the flowing motion draws the chi up and fills, refills, and refreshes the entire body.

The entire warm-up commitment here facilitates the gentle inclusion of these two inner states of awareness as you engage in the activities in your life. Generally these activities can be done at any time, any place, without drawing unwanted attention. Standing, sitting, even lying down, they are adaptable to all situations

Moving from your hips and letting the motion flow throughout your body as you breathe is the beginning. So start in your kitchen, reach for the cup from your hips, and let your chi start to do what it was meant to do: bring you health and a state of well-being that is not dependant on life's outer experiences. They already exist because they exist in the chi already in you.

There are several other tips on moving and relaxation that can also support your interest in finally learning the actual T'ai Chi sequences. Let's continue progressing with our warm-ups.

Nature Walk

To continue to help open up your body movement initiating at the hips, try the Nature Walk. This can be done anywhere at any time. To do this, think of the tail of an animal, bird, or reptile of your choice. You might pick it for its beauty, strength, or agility—any tail you choose is fine. Now imagine it is attached to you, directly on your tail bone and as you walk you are dragging it along behind you. Walk with this imagined tail coming along behind you. This mental picture creates an awakening of the nerves in the tailbone (perhaps because it wasn't so long ago we actually did have a tail), and the energy flows of the sacrum and the tan t'ien are refreshed

> Relaxation in the highest sense means faith.
> —Lawrence Galante

and aligned. This supports the increasing vitality associated with heightening chi reserves. And the awakening of this area promotes movement, in this case walking, generated from the hip and pelvis. Any walking or movement you do that opens the gentle movement of the lower portion of your body is a positive step in the course you have set.

This walk is an absolutely wonderful tool that accomplishes several things. First, you learn better the body concept of how to move your legs while doing T'ai Chi. It is so valuable that it can be done any time at all. It will improve your skill at balancing and you will find your center of balance becoming more firmly established in your tan t'ien. You will calm your mind and feelings by focusing yourself on your steps, and it can easily be moved into a quiet, slow walking meditation. There is really no reason not to practice this often. If your balance is a little sketchy, then place yourself next to a steady support and use that. You may find it is more to your liking to take very small steps at first. This is fine. It really doesn't matter if you cover ground at all. It is the empty-full leg concept that yields the most gifts here. So relax, take a stroll down a path, next to a wall, or between two chairs.

In the following Nature Walk exercise, bring your tail right along into this walk. It will position the lower back correctly and help with balance.

NATURE WALK

Standing, relax into your form.

Let the string draw you erect. Your torso is light, your lower half is stable, and your weight is evenly distributed between left and right and front and back. To achieve this, rock very slightly from side to side until you find your perfect balance point.

Then rock ever so slightly from front to back and find your balance point again.

They will be one and the same and form a plumb line of central balance for you.

Very naturally slide your right leg forward a comfortable step. Not too far. As your right foot slides into place, begin to shift your weight into your right leg.

When you can, shift your left foot out about forty-five degrees. Seventy percent of your weight will be in your right leg and foot and thirty percent will be in your left.

Sink down into your tail and left leg.
Your right leg is extended but the weight
is changing.
Your right heel is now barely touching
the ground.
All of your weight is in your left leg and
your right leg is completely empty.

Lightly press your right toe into the
ground.
Shift your weight from the full left leg into
the now filling right leg.
Your back is straight and you are balanced
between your two legs.

All your weight has now shifted to the right leg.

Your left leg bends, completely empty.

Lift the heel and then the toe.

One hundred percent of your weight is in your right leg.

Step right on through with your empty left leg.

Left heel touches the floor first, then the toe lies down.

Now shift your weight seventy percent in the back right leg and thirty percent in your front left leg.

Continue now, mirroring the walk on the other side.

The next movement is done when leaning over. It doesn't matter if you need to support or balance yourself when you lean over or not. Any way you bend is fine. When you are ready to straighten up, you are ready to move on to the next exercise.

Sprouting

Imagine (again) that you have a sprout growing straight up through the center of your spine. It is the sprout that brings you erect from the bending position of the previous warm-up and now replaces the suspending string. The muscles actually can once again begin to relax in your form as you become erect through the efforts of the sprout, not your muscles. This simple exercise of your mind and body allows your body to use your muscles more correctly. And the benefit of this is more inner tranquility as well as preparing your spine for the freedom of the movements.

Relaxation the T'ai Chi way is a great experience. Usually when we relax, we lie prone or sit. We alter our awareness with daydreams or lose awareness (sleep) altogether. We let go of our body awareness and relax. In T'ai Chi deep relaxation is felt while you are standing and present, not daydreaming. Although complete inner relaxation while standing is the traditional goal, this can also then apply to sitting or lying. This is often daunting, particularly if you have a few little glitches that make relaxing in your form a bit uncomfortable. Not to worry. You will find your own type of relaxing within the form, lying prone, sitting, or even standing. This exercise may help.

Stress to Sand

Lying prone, sitting, or standing feel the sensation of your skin as it touches clothing, air, floor, furniture, wherever and whatever it is touching you right now. Think of your skin as a sack in which you live. Starting at the top of your spine, the occipital, imagine that sand is beginning to flow out of this joint, just like sand draining through your fingers. Imagine all of your tension morphing into sand—carrying with it all the tension within your head—and just draining down and out. This tension transformed into sand drains out of your neck, down and across your shoulders to the shoulder joint, the elbow joint, wrist, thumb and finger joints—all of your tension is draining now as sand. The sand falls downward and disappears into the floor. The sand now begins to pour out of the vertebrae, heading on down to your sacrum, across the hip joints, pouring through the hip and out the knee joints, ankles, foot, and toe joints. So you are now draining sand, allowing the feeling of being relaxed within your form. If you

> With regular practice your mind will be less likely to wander and your memory may improve since you need to remember each movement and form in the sequence.... It can even sharpen your thinking.
> —Wu Yue Sun, William Chen

are lying or sitting, get comfortable with this method of reducing joint tension and muscle stress and then give it a try standing. It will allow you to nudge up closer to relaxing the T'ai Chi way.

Practice these casual warm-ups, invite them into you everyday, and feel their great benefits of relaxation and well-being. Once you become comfortable with these exercises, you'll be well on your way to a life of T'ai Chi. Let's continue now with some of the "classic" warm-ups we mentioned earlier.

Classic Style Warm-ups

The second type of warm-up is the classic T'ai Chi warm-up. These are required to create the receptive flexibility needed to start a T'ai Chi practice session.

PELVIC ROLLS

Place your feet about shoulder width apart. Place your hands, fingers down, at the base of your spine. Now roll your hips, without forcing. You can imagine rolling your hips around the inside of a barrel. Or, some like the hula image. Roll first to the left, then to the right.

KNEE ROLLS

Place your feet together and bend your knees slightly.

Place your palms on your knees, fingers toward the inside.

Roll your knees to the front and then to the left side, back (they will straighten slightly), to the right, and then back to the front.

Do this with the knees only slightly bent, don't force.

You will feel your weight shifting slightly on the soles of your feet. Your ankles, knees, and hips will all move in a circular motion. This exercise begins to create flexibility in the legs and get them ready for the T'ai Chi movements.

ANKLE ROLLS

Stabilize yourself as needed, and pick up one leg and rotate the ankle in both directions.

Replace that foot securely under your body and lift the other to roll that ankle. This is a perfect place to practice your yang, full leg, and your yin, empty leg.

Neck Rolls

Just as it sounds—roll your head on your shoulders. To the front, to the left, to the back, and to the right. Repeat in the other direction.

The neck is tricky. A whole lot goes on there, and in T'ai Chi you don't actually move the head a lot. Mainly you just keep your head suspended upward. So in rolling the neck, be very light. Don't go further than is comfortable. If you are lightheaded, don't roll the head to the back at all and have something to hold onto in case you lose your balance for a second.

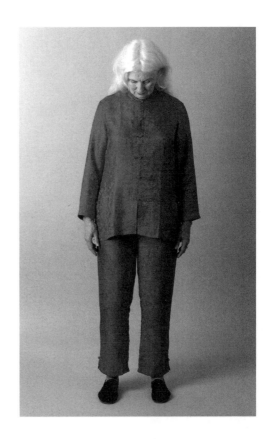

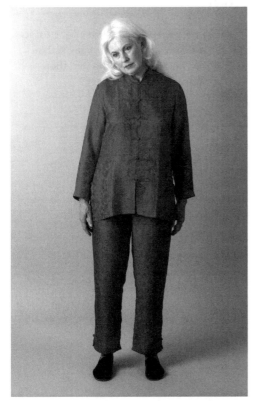

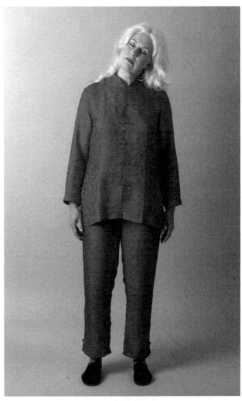

Soft Chest

Let your arms hang to the side.
Let the lower half of your body become
full of your weight.
Let the upper torso become light.
Let all the heaviness in your chest drain
downward (remember the sand) into
your pelvis, hips, legs, and feet.
Touch your sternum and let all the holding,
lifting up, and tightness just let go into
the heavy lower body.

Waist Rolls

Hands on your waist, roll this light torso
on your now very heavy, very stable
legs and hips. First to the left, then
to the right.

Wide Stance

Place your feet a bit further than shoulder width apart, hands hanging to your side at about seamline. Soften your chest, suspend your head on the string, relax your shoulders, and let your upper body relax into the great stability of your lower half. Imagine your lower half is like a mountain under you, and completely let go into its stability.

Basic Leg Warm-ups

The base of this activity is, of course, the legs. There is a particular emphasis on the legs that is very T'ai Chi. The stability of the legs is increased with two basic ideas. The first idea is the concept of empty-full. The second idea is the concept of seventy percent-thirty percent.

The first concept, empty-full, is rooted in the philosophical belief of yin, the empty, and yang, the full. These two forces of yin and yang are symbolized by and are believed to be the essential components of chi. Yin, the empty, is also known as the feminine force of energy, while yang, the full, is known as the masculine force of energy. To have lasting vitality and durable longevity, it is essential that the two forces that comprise chi be balanced as this vital force courses through the body. In T'ai Chi the legs are deeply engaged in the ongoing attainment of both physical and energetic balance. Throughout T'ai Chi they work in concert with each other. While one is full—heavy and weight-bearing—the other is empty—light and free to move easily. The legs alternate back and forth, exchanging empty-full and full-empty. This exchange constitutes fertile practice.

Again, this practice can be accomplished in a designated environment at a particular time or you can fit it into your everyday routines at will. The idea is to shift the weight in your legs back and forth. Quite simple. This is best done slowly so you can feel the subtleties in the movement. Sand again becomes an interesting concept to work with. Shift your weight as you are reading this to your right leg. This is best accomplished standing, but can also be easily done sitting. Imagine that sand, like the sand in an hourglass, is pouring into the right leg and the leg is becoming fuller and fuller, until it is fully weighted by the sand. Now in comparison, your left leg can become lighter and emptier. Emptier and emptier until, when weighted on the right leg, you feel as if you could guide the left leg's movements effortlessly. Now feel the sand shift again, this time out of the right leg and into the left. The left leg begins to heavy up as the right becomes ever lighter. There comes a moment when each leg is equally weighted and your torso is balanced perfectly between the two legs. You can pause here and practice the shifting of

> Because the T'ai Chi form excludes extreme movement and emphasizes gradualness in learning, its practitioners avoid pulled muscles and other injuries that sometimes accompany more strenuous activity. . .a feeling of restraint is encouraged and no movement is ever forced.
> —Herman Kauz

the feet, or you can continue on over to the left leg, feeling the alternating patterns that occur as the right leg becomes heavy.

This shifting from one to the other, done in a gentle, flowing fashion, is the early leg patterning for the basic T'ai Chi leg moves. These basic moves then become more effective in initiating and supporting the movement in the upper body by becoming what is generally known as seventy percent-thirty percent. What this means is during the course of the T'ai Chi movements the legs move slowly from empty to full, yin to yang, and in this way they also stabilize and sustain balance by becoming at times seventy percent full in one leg while the other is thirty percent full.

Take a moment to familiarize yourself with how this feels. Find a sense of seventy percent full in the leg of your choice and bring the thirty percent full to the other leg. Now, without moving your feet, switch. (The seventy percent will feel heavier than the thirty percent.) The seventy percent leg becomes thirty percent. The thirty percent leg is now seventy percent full. This subtle balance shift is attained by moving your torso slightly from one leg to the other. A small shift is sufficient.

When the shifting, filling state of seventy percent-thirty percent is familiar, then take a step, one foot forward about the distance of only a foot and the other foot remains in the same place. In moving your foot position there are a few important points to keep in mind.

1. Keep a completely stable yang leg, hold it rooted.
2. Move your completely empty yin leg and take a small step with it.
3. If stepping to the side, don't step beyond your shoulder.
4. When taking a step to the front, do not let the knee go beyond the ankle when the foot touches the ground.
5. When stepping to the back, let your foot fall at a comfortable angle just a bit behind, and then gently shift your weight back. No big steps at all. The entire sequence is done within a small space.
6. The moving leg is always yin. The steady, stabilizing leg is always yang.

Have you found your own seventy percent-thirty percent ratio in your legs? If so, we can develop the step further. We are still working with seventy percent-thirty percent and the difference is that the feet will now move. The moving leg will be the empty leg, or the yin leg. The stable leg will be the full, or yang, leg.

Let your left leg become empty as your right leg fills to full. Easily move your left leg to the side, under your shoulder, and now the left becomes seventy percent full and the right is lightened to thirty percent. Hold steady. Now let the right leg become completely empty as the left leg (now yang) stabilizes the movement as it heavies up. As your left leg anchors, your right leg easily and lightly moves forward about a foot. For movement, the legs are yin and yang. For stances or standing still, the legs are seventy percent-thirty percent.

Now play with this concept. Move slowly, a small step to the side or in front. Take a step to the front, letting the knee bend slightly and keeping the knee directly over the forward moved foot. As you take the different stances, vary the seventy percent leg and the thirty percent leg. You can also go completely yin and yang by moving through the various stances with alternating full and empty legs.

Make sure you are not stressing your knees and make sure you choose a teacher who is cognizant of this and reminds you if you misalign a bit.

From the moment we were born we have possessed instinctive desires for food, comfort, affections, and other pleasures. These desires grow stronger and multiply as the baby becomes a child, and the child becomes the adult. They could be endless in the pursuit of our goals in friendship, love, marriage, wealth and success, or just merely of a chance to survive in famine or war...
It's slow and gentle movements act to "lubricate" every part of our body and relax the mind. This ancient system renders our thinking lucid, turns our temper gentle and brings us into peace of mind that helps us to function well in our hectic modern world—whether in education, career, or social relations.
—William C.C. Chen

FORWARD LEG SEVENTY PERCENT
BACK LEG THIRTY PERCENT

FORWARD LEG THIRTY PERCENT
BACK LEG SEVENTY PERCENT

FULL ON RIGHT (YANG)
EMPTY ON LEFT (YIN)

FULL ON LEFT (YANG)
EMPTY ON RIGHT (YIN)

Chapter 11

The Sequence

This book is filled with words describing all aspects of chi, T'ai Chi, and Qigong. But now we'll begin learning the physical form, so the words will be sparse. With the following series of yang form T'ai Chi try to achieve a sense of flow with the movements. Follow the pictures for the basic positions and the written instructions for descriptions of moving from one position to the next. While practicing, try to concentrate on your legs and feet, keeping your awareness on empty, full, and seventy percent-thirty percent. Your upper body will float, light as a butterfly, in the various positions as your focus is on the stability in your legs and feet and the graceful lightness of your upper body. Your waist is the melting middle of the two. Pliable and agile, the waist enables the upper and lower to merge in gentle, supportive harmony.

You may find it easiest to read the very simple instructions and then put them onto an audio tape. Find your spot, turn on the audio tape, relax into the form, and begin. What is important is not the perfection of your form, but the new body rhythm you are integrating. A rhythm of shifting with stability—a heavy lower half, a loose and pliable waist, and a floating, defined grace on top. This is the goal. If you take the time to record the basic instructions in a slow, easy-to-follow rhythm, you will enhance this step in your T'ai Chi process.

Remember:

- Take your time
- Take small steps
- Keep your feet solid
- Let your arms float
- Let your waist be soft
- Enjoy!

The Sequence

Learning T'ai Chi from an instructor is essential but for those of you who live where this is simply not possible, I have adjusted the usual yang short form to support the yang form taught in the beautifully illustrated book, *A Beginner's Guide to Tai Chi* by Ray Pawlett.

The illustrations here are clear, profuse, and will provide an adequate T'ai Chi experience for you until you can find a teacher.

> Your body can
> be light and agile.

OPENING THE FORM

POSITION 1
Relax your mind
Place your feet at shoulder width
Relax your joints—
    Knees soft
    Shoulders down
    Head extended from the string
    Spine extending
    Hands and elbows relaxed
    Waist relaxed
    Upper body light
    Lower body heavy
    Feet nestled into sand
The base of your spine cups the tan t'ien

POSITION 2
Extend your fingers straight
Relax your shoulders
Your elbows are heavy and straight
Lift your hands

POSITION 3
Extend your arms, as if they are
    floating on water
Your legs are heavy
Your upper body is light

POSITION 4
Relax your shoulders
Sink your elbows and draw your
    forearms back
Your hands point upward at your
    shoulders

POSITION 5
Your shoulders are relaxed
Your elbows are heavy
Press your flat palms toward earth

WARD OFF LEFT

POSITION 6
Soften your waist
Rotate clockwise
Your right hand draws back
Your left hand floats forward
Turn your right foot out forty-five percent
Right leg seventy percent
Left leg thirty percent

POSITION 7
Bring your left leg forward, toe up,
    heel down
Pretend you're holding a large, imaginary
    ball with your right hand on top, left on
    the bottom
Your weight is entirely on right leg
Right leg yang
Left leg yin

POSITION 8
Loosen your waist
Your right hand moves up, with your
    elbow heavy
Your left hand float, extended beyond
    your right hand
Left leg thirty percent
Right leg seventy percent

POSITION 9
Your right arm floats downward
Your left arm floats upward
Right leg seventy percent
Left leg thirty percent

GRASPING SPARROW'S TAIL

POSITION 10
Your left foot turns out forty-five degrees
Hold your big, imaginary ball—left arm
    above, right arm below
Right leg yang
Left leg yin

POSITION 11
Relax your shoulders
Relax your elbows
Left leg yang
Right leg yin

POSITION 12
Step forward with your empty right leg
Your left leg stays yang
Let the heel of your right foot come
    to floor
Your hands remain as before

POSITION 13
Push weight from your left leg
Receive weight in your right leg
Your left hand wards off your floating arm
Your right hand moves to support your
    floating arm

POSITION 14
Soften your waist
Rotate clockwise
Your elbows are heavy
Your shoulders are relaxed
Your arms reach forward
Right leg seventy percent
Left leg thirty percent

POSITION 15
Soften your waist
Rotate counterclockwise
Your elbows are heavy
Your hands draw back
Left leg seventy percent
Right leg thirty percent

POSITION 16
Turn to face center
Your left palm moves to your inner
    right wrist
Left leg yang
Right leg yin

POSITION 17
Your arm position expands
Right leg seventy percent
Left leg thirty percent

POSITION 18
Your arms press forward, floating
Extend chi into your arms
Right leg seventy percent
Left leg thirty percent

POSITION 19
Return your waist to center alignment
Your arms are extended, relaxed
Your fingers are separated
Right leg seventy percent
Left leg thirty percent

POSITION 20
Sink your shoulders
Drop your elbows
Your hands float up
Left leg yang
Right leg yin

POSITION 21
Your hands push forward
Your elbows are heavy
Right leg seventy percent
Left leg thirty percent

POSITION 22
Push forward from your left heel
Push through your body
Right leg seventy percent
Left leg thirty percent

SINGLE WHIP

POSITION 23
Drop your elbows
Your hands move up
Center your waist
Return your body to center
Right foot thirty percent
Left foot seventy percent

POSITION 24
Turn your waist to face the back corner
Your weight is balanced on both feet

POSITION 25
Turn your waist clockwise
Your shoulders relax
Your elbows are heavy
Your hands drawn up

Position 26
Push to the corner
Right leg seventy percent
Left leg thirty percent

Position 27
Hold the whip with your right hand, your
    arm floats
Your left hand turns at your collar
Right leg yang
Left leg yin

POSITION **28**
Pushing your weight from
   right leg seventy percent to
   left leg thirty percent
Your hand is moved forward

POSITION **29**
Your body is centered

RAISE HANDS

POSITION 30
Hold a big, imaginary ball, hands facing
    each other
Right leg yang
Left foot outward forty-five degrees

POSITION 31
Turn your waist counterclockwise
Center yourself
Close your hands
Left leg seventy percent
Right leg thirty percent

POSITION 32
Right leg yin
Sit into left leg
Draw your hands together,
    left below right
Your fingers stretched forward

POSITION 33
Move your hands forward, right before
    left, and level with your right elbow
Your spine is straight
Left leg yang
Right leg yin, heel touching

POSITION 34
Move your right palm down
Move your left palm up
Right leg yin, heel down

POSITION 35
Right leg yin, steps forward
Your heel touches
Lower your right hand
Raise your left hand

POSITION 36
Press your weight into your right leg
Your forearms are parallel
Your hands are facing each other
Right leg seventy percent
Left leg thirty percent

POSITION 37
Raise your right arm
Lower your left arm
Your hands are touching, your right palm
    against the back of your left hand.
Right yang
Left yin

POSITION 38
Your arms separate
Raise your right arm and lower your
    left arm
Your palms face toward the earth
Right leg yang
Left leg yin

WHITE CRANE SPREADS ITS WINGS

POSITION 39
Move your weight into right leg
Press to the earth with your left hand
Press to heaven with your right hand
Right leg yang
Left leg yin

Position 40
Move your shoulders down
Float your right arm down
Right leg yang
Left leg yin

Position 41
Your right elbow gets heavy and
    draws your arm back
Your left arm moves in front of
    your body
Right leg seventy percent
Left leg thirty percent

POSITION 42
With your left leg yin, step forward
Your right palm draws back, ready for
   the press
Your left hand is poised and floating

BRUSH AND PUSH

POSITION 43
Move your right hand into the press
Your left hand moves down, palm facing
   the earth, your elbow relaxed
Left leg seventy percent
Right leg thirty percent

POSITION 44
Your right hand continues to push
Your left hand still presses to the earth
Left leg seventy percent
Right leg thirty percent

POSITION 45
Extend right hand—hand to earth
Left hand facing in, elbow heavy
Left leg yang
Right leg yin

STRUM THE LUTE

POSITION 46
Turn your body to the left
Raise your right arm so that it is
    straight out from your shoulder
Raise your left arm, elbow bent, so
    that your left hand is level with
    your shoulder
Place your hands as if they are strumming
    a lute
Right leg yang
Left leg yin

BRUSH AND PUSH

POSITION 47
Turn your body to the left
Lower your left arm so that your palm is
    level with and facing your chest
Lower your right arm and twist it back
Right leg seventy percent
Left leg thirty percent

BRUSH AND PUSH

POSITION 48

Press and push your left hand forward

Raise and draw back your right hand, palm
   facing forward and level with your
   shoulder

Right foot seventy percent

Left foot thirty percent

POSITION 49

Pull back your left arm, bending at your
   elbow, your left palm is flat to Earth

Your right hand pushes forward

Left foot seventy percent

Right foot thirty percent

BRUSH AND PUSH

POSITION 50
Right leg yang
Left leg yin, turned out forty-five degrees
Pull back your right arm so that your right
  palm is ready for a push
Your left palm is lowered to the earth

POSITION 51
Left leg seventy percent
Right leg thirty percent
Move your hands so that they are level
  in front of your stomach and ready for
  a push

POSITION 52
Left leg yang
Right leg yin
Extend your right foot forward
Your hands start to push

POSITION 53
Left leg thirty percent
Right leg seventy percent
Press your left hand forward
Lower your right hand toward the earth

POSITION 54

Left leg yang: sink your weight into the leg

Right leg yin: turn out your toes

Bring your left hand back, bending your elbow, so that it is at collar level

Move your right hand so that it is descending down at thigh level, your right palm turns to face your center

POSITION 55

Right leg seventy percent

Left leg thirty percent

Lower your left hand and turn your palm to face the earth

Right hand floats up and follows the movement of the left hand

POSITION 56
Right leg yang
Left leg yin
Step through with your left leg
Move your right hand up, palm forward
Extend and lower your left hand toward
the earth

POSITION 57
Left foot seventy percent
Right foot thirty percent
Your right hand begins the push, palm
facing forward
Draw back your left hand, palm facing
forward

STRUM THE GUITAR

POSITION 58
Left leg seventy percent
Right leg thirty percent
Press your right hand into the push
Draw back your left hand, palm facing
forward

PLAY THE GUITAR

POSITION 59
Left leg seventy percent
Right leg thirty percent
Turn your body slightly to the right
Your right hand stays extended in
the push
Lower your left hand, palm facing
the earth

POSITION 60
Right leg yang
Left leg yin
Turn slightly to the left
Your right hand draws up and back
Your left hand extends, fingers relaxed,
   palms facing toward you

POSITION 61
Right leg yang
Left leg yin: step forward
With your left arm bent, raise your
   fingers up so that your hand is level
   with your face
Lower your right hand and move it
   forward toward your left elbow

BRUSH AND PUSH

POSITION 62
Right leg yang
Left leg yin: step forward
Extend your right arm and move it back
Lower your left hand so that your arm is
   level with your shoulder, palm facing
   toward you

POSITION 63
Right leg seventy percent
Left leg thirty percent
Raise your right arm, elbow bent, so your
   hand is level with your chin and your
   palm faces forward
Your left arm lowers and extends, palm
   slightly curved toward the earth

PARRY

POSITION 64
Right leg seventy percent
Left leg thirty percent
Press your right hand forward
Draw back your left arm

POSITION 65
Right leg yang
Left leg yin
Move both hands to meet directly in front
  of your chest
Make a loose fist with your right hand
  makes loose fit
Your left hand cradles the right

POSITION 66
Left leg seventy percent
Right leg thirty percent
Extend your right hand forward, hand still
in a fist
Lower your left hand, palm facing up
Press down with both hands

POSITION 67
Left leg yang
Right leg yin: step through
Move your hands along with your legs

POSITION 68
Left leg seventy percent
Right leg thirty percent
Turn slightly to the right
Raise and push your left hand
Lower your right fist

POSITION 69
Right leg thirty percent
Left leg seventy percent
Draw back your right fist
Extend your left arm as your left hand
  blocks

POSITION 70
Right leg yang
Left leg yin, step through
Continue to press with your left hand
Your right hand remains in a loose fist

POSITION 71
Right leg seventy percent
Left leg thirty percent
Move your right arm forward as if your
    fist punches
Draw back and raise your left hand, palm
    open and facing forward

POSITION 72
Left leg seventy percent
Right leg thirty percent
Your right hand finishes the punch
Your left hand moves to protect your
right elbow

EXTEND AND PUSH

POSITION 73
Left leg seventy percent
Right leg thirty percent
Your right hand opens and faces
toward heaven
Your left hand supports your right elbow

POSITION **74**
Right leg seventy percent
Left leg thirty percent
Twist your waist to the right
Draw your right hand back
Push your left hand forward

POSITION **75**
Right leg yang
Left leg yin
Drop both of your elbows
Draw your left hand back
Ready both hands for the press

POSITION 76
Right leg seventy percent
Left leg thirty percent
Press through with both hands from your
    right heel

CLOSING THE FORM

POSITION 77
Right leg seventy percent
Left leg thirty percent, turn toes in
Spread your arms as if to hold big ball,
    palms facing your center

POSITION 78
Right leg yang
Left leg yin
Spread your arms as if the ball is
    now bigger
Move your palms to face outward

POSITION 79
Left leg yang
Right leg yin
Return to beginning stance
Bring hands back to your center, your
    palms face toward you and cross over
    each other

POSITION 80
Move your feet so that they are parallel
Your weight is even
Your forearms remain crossed

POSITION 81
Extend your arms
Open your hands, your palms facing
   toward heaven
Your head is being lifted on the string
Your spine is extending from your head

POSITION 82
Turn palms down, facing toward the earth
Your shoulders are relaxed

POSITION 83
Your shoulders are relaxed
Bend your arms at the elbows and lower
    them to be level with your stomach
Turn your palms down and press to the
    floor

POSITION **84**
Stand relaxed and feel the effect of the
   movements

You have just completed your first practice of T'ai Chi movements. Be patient with yourself as you learn each step. With practice these movements will become smooth and fluid. Enjoy the wonderful feelings T'ai Chi will bring to you.

Every movement of T'ai Chi Ch'uan is expressed from Wu-Chi to T'ai Chi, or from preconsciousness to actual internal consciousness. Movement is never initiated merely by the hands, arms, or legs. Instead, the mind itself directs the body to function as a single unit, with every joint linked. The body should be agile and natural; the movement, continuous and constant, like a mountain spring flowing increasingly into the stream. The concept of body unity is delicately intertwined with the very important principle of moving the body continuously.

—Master Juo, Tsung Hwa

Part Five

Enriching Your Daily Life with T'ai Chi

Chapter 12

Chi Exercises

As you progress in your T'ai Chi practice, you'll find that many of the exercises and principles can aid in your everyday life. This chapter will focus on some very valuable chi breaks available to you. Each one is easy to do once it is familiar. And since chi follows thought or intent, once you become familiar with it, you can put it in place immediately just by thinking about it. Here are some simple chi exercises you can use to improve your everyday life:

1. *Someone Has Irritated You and You Start to Respond*
   Remember, the more irritated you are, the harsher the chi. This harsh chi speeds up the aging process in the body. Your chi exercise to correct this is to bend your knees slightly, press your feet into the ground, and inhale earth chi up and exhale universal chi down.

2. *You are Feeling Heavy and Stressed and Your Life Weighs Heavily*
   Press your feet to the earth and soften your knees. Inhale, and fill up as deeply as your body will allow. Through slightly-parted lips let the weight in your upper body sink. Sink down from the head and shoulders, through the torso, and fill up the lower half. As you breathe in and out, your upper body becomes lighter and lighter and your lower body is heavy and anchored. You will feel more balanced and renewed within your life.

3. *Your Mind is Racing*
   Bring your awareness to your legs. Put all your weight on one leg and let the other become completely empty. One is the anchor and the other is completely light and empty. Now, by slowly shifting your weight, reverse the heavy leg and the light leg. See how subtle you can be in these movements.

Focus entirely on this full-empty process. After a few minutes, return from your chi exercise to your thoughts. They will be slower and you will be in better control of your inner life.

4. *Your Energy Level Has Hit Bottom*
Do the pre-birth breath for five minutes.

5. *You Need an Extra Jolt of Energy*
Put your hands, fingers laced, over the tan t'ien (about one inch below your navel). Inhale, breathe the earth up. Exhale the universe down. Stay focused on chi settling to the tan t'ien. Feel the chi begin to build as you feel warmth and aliveness throughout your pelvis. Take a big breath, draw the chi up, and disperse it throughout your body. Your body will now be better energized and more grounded.

6. *You are Sitting Somewhere, Stressed*
Relax your belly. Relax your tan t'ien. Let the air breathe you. Expand, and the air flows in. Relax and let the air flow out all on its own. Let your jaw relax down and then back. Your lips may part. You are vital and relaxed, so relaxed that the air is breathing you.

7. *The Hustle of Life is Making You Nuts*
Place your fingertips lightly on your tan t'ien. Sink your breath to the tan t'ien. Hold your breath very briefly, exhale, and let the tension throughout your upper body disperse with the exhaled breath. You are actually ridding yourself of the harsher chi and replacing it with a smoother, more refined chi. This will, in turn, bring you a better feeling of being placid amidst the haste. To enhance this encouraging state of events further, gently tug on your ears from the tops to the lobes. Take a deep breath and gently raise your arms up, cross them over your chest, and put your hands around the back of your neck. Now, take a small step back and gently release your breath. Release your arms down to your sides. This chi breath accomplishes two important things. First, it refines your chi, and second, it provides an energetic boundary between you and the hustle and bustle.

8. *Take Charge of Your Responses*
So often it is possible to view people responding to the same thing entirely differently. One has a kind smile, the other peevish impatience. Both people are exhibiting emotions that are the result of how they pull chi from the field around them. The chi field, in constant availability, fills a person according to the yin-yang balance they, with their intent, draw to themselves on their breath. One drew in chi and it stayed softer and refined. The other drew in chi and it became harsh and irritating. Using these chi breaks until

they become a completely integrated part of your life can give you a welcome tool for establishing responses that serve you and others consistently.

9. *T'ai Chi and Qigong as Tools*

It is not at all necessary to do the full short yang form of T'ai Chi or a full round of Qigong to benefit from a movement. It is important to do T'ai Chi each day. This is true for Qigong as well. But once done, they become allies during the day, ready and waiting to be accessed as needed. You step into the form as you do T'ai Chi. You make a conscious decision to enter a chi field that has been set before you, and you set yourself now with T'ai Chi and Qigong movements. This quiet and refined field is the form of T'ai Chi and Qigong and it can be present and useful for you most anywhere life becomes a tangle. You can avail yourself of this chi field as you do T'ai Chi and Qigong, of course, but you can also draw it to yourself in quick and effective ways.

- Think of doing the form, and breathe as if you are already doing it.
- Move, just one movement appropriate to where you are, using the T'ai Chi form.
- Evolve your head upward and let your upper body drain into your lower body.
- Breathe and let your chest be as light as possible.
- Do the first steps in the form, finding your perfect balance, and rest in the balance between the right and left sides.
- Remember a favorite quote from an ancient master. Turn it over and over in your mind. Apply the wisdom to your own life events.
- Turn using your hips to initiate the motion.

Keep a clear understanding that taking any snippet from T'ai Chi and inserting it into your life as needed, will encourage your own creativity. Over time you will find your own favorite T'ai Chi and Qigong mini movements.

10. *To Build Steadiness*

This works for emotional and physical steadiness. Let your eyes rest on something, one thing. Or pick a spot somewhere to watch. As your eyes gaze steadily, let natural breath take over your body, a steady flow in and out as your relaxed and steady gaze never falters. Letting the lower half of your body heavy-up helps with this as well.

11. *To Regain Perspective*

Let your lower half be heavy. Touch your tan t'ien lightly and briefly, drop your breath to the tan t'ien, and look to the horizon. Look to the sky. Look to the clouds. Then look back to the horizon. Feel your breath flowing into you and out of you all the way from and to the farthest horizon and beyond. Let your breath move naturally and deeply within you. Feel the breath sink to the tan t'ien, and draw your breath from the farthest horizon.

12. *To Maximize Focus*

Step into your T'ai Chi form and put all of your attention on the movement. Place your thoughts into the movement. Align your breath with the movement.

13. *Focusing and Calming the Mind*

Locate a part of your body that seems out of balance, tense, tired, etc. Breathe through your nose and imagine the breath moving into your lump of tension or tiredness. Let this part of your body receive the air. You are directing chi with your mind. Keep breathing into this area. Let it feel as if it is expanding, softening, settling down, draining down. When the draining feeling is in place, then try moving just that muscle area. Tense and relax; breathe; tense and exhale; relax and inhale.

14. *Making Your Hands Warmer*

Put your hands together and slowly move them apart. See if you can feel chi currents flowing between your hands. Bring your hands together and then apart a bit, about one inch when close and six inches when apart. You might feel a gentle pressure, a bit like holding a bubble with a lot of surface tension between your hands. Keep rolling it around. Try pulling your hands father apart and see when it becomes harder to feel. Then draw them back together, noticing when the "bubble" makes itself known again. Breathe into your hands, directing chi into them. The flows and the bubble may become easier and easier to discover. Play with this. You might think about what color these flows and this bubble might be. Let your hands rest, palms down, in your lap.

15. *Warming and Enlivening the Feet*

Just your good, old basic foot massage is a good start here. While giving them a good rubdown, feel for the "gate" on the foot. Place your pointer finger between the big toe and the second toe next to it. Draw your finger up your foot. Just as you arrive at the base of the bump on the top of the foot, your finger will find a little spot it fits into perfectly. This is the acupressure point for releasing the earth flow into the body. Massage this point by making small circles in the indentation. Now hold onto each big toe containing it as best you can. Breathe chi through the hands and into the feet. Imagine your feet are becoming more and more relaxed, expanded, even fluffy, like clouds. Often another massage is good. This takes a while, but it is worth it because you are enlivening your feet. After these treatments, they will not only be warmer, but they will also be more sensitive to pleasure.

16. *Stressed and Sensitive Eyes*
The T'ai Chi masters walked in the dew each morning before their practice to strengthen the eyes. Then they would do T'ai Chi in the emerging sunrise. It seems mysterious, but the ancient claim is worth investigating, particularly if your new sleep cycle gives you an early morning wake-up time.

17. *Another Eye Refresher*
Cup your palms over your eyes in such a way that no light is visible to your open eye. Relax your eyes. (Open or closed is your call.) Breathe chi into your hands and direct it with your mind through your palms, and into your eyes. Imagine your eyes are two globes floating in a vast, deep space. Feel the globes, not pressing against your eyelids, but instead deep within your head. Floating and filling with refined chi directed by your thoughts. You may want to support your elbows to get more comfortable. Now let your eyes float deep in your head, floating on smooth chi.

18. *Getting an Acknowledged "No"*
When you are having trouble getting someone to hear you say no, use your chi. You can keep your voice at the same level, even quieter, only this time when you say no, direct your chi out of your tan t'ien toward the resisting person. It is like a stream of strength flowing out, gently but firmly delivering its message to the person as you say your no one last time. It works. Try it.

> Think of your mind as a T.V. You can focus on one channel or channel surf. For T'ai Chi switch to a quiet, soothing channel.

19. *Staying Grounded*
Not being grounded can cause poor balance, headaches, unnecessary business, lack of attention to detail, not listening. . .and the list goes on. As you inhale, receive chi coming up from Earth. It is a gift to you. You need only to open to receive it. As you exhale, receive the gift of the Universal energy coming down into you. Place your attention on your tan t'ien. Take a space for yourself. Breathe and keep focused on the tan t'ien. This will ground you and help relieve stress symptoms.

20. *It Has Been a Tiring Day*
Your body is tired and just lying down is your deepest desire. You stretch out and sink in. Just lie there and make one small shift in your awareness before you completely relax. Let the fatigue start to draw out of you like the

exercise Stress to Sand on pages 105–106. Down, down, down it drains. And now here is the important addition: As the fatigue/sand drains out of your muscles, bones, and joints, you feel your body becoming lighter and lighter. Not more energized, but lighter. Continue to relax. The sand drains, you feel lighter and lighter. Now really burrow into your relaxation. As you rest, the chi is free to circulate. Fatigue can make chi very sluggish. This prevents deep relaxation and interferes with a satisfying night's rest. Remember to refine your chi before you completely let go of the day, and you will reap valuable rewards.

21. *A Chi Eye*

Is there a part of your body that feels stiff? Perhaps it is the same part of your body that is slow to "get," let alone master, a T'ai Chi movement. The back is a particularly good candidate for this. Let's say lower back. Try a chi eye. Imagine you have an eye in the lower back. You aren't moving a stiff and resistant back. Instead you are moving an eye back and forth. This is a sensing eye rather than a seeing eye. Your focus is to move the back to give the eye lots to sense. It may seem like an odd idea, but try it. When you narrow the focus to one area, the muscles will move to support this area. Chi flows into a freed-up area and the muscles work in improved harmony and, in this case, your lower back is looser and freer in its movement.

Chapter 13

Meditation and the Meditative Environment

Meditation usually conjures up an image of a person sitting cross-legged on a pillow, spine straight and eyes closed. Because each person is unique, one type of meditation for everyone is too limiting. A meditation style that works perfectly for one will not be a good tool at all for another. T'ai Chi and Qigong provide excellent gateways for meditation.

All types of meditation are committed to the same outcome: the reduction of tension between the body's desires and the soul's nature. The route for this balance is the conscious receiving and directing of chi. In sitting meditation the chi is directed into a still body. In T'ai Chi and Qigong the chi is directed as a part of the movement. Understanding chi and receiving and directing it are the keys to opening an entire world of awareness, health, and well-being. To know chi is to begin to grasp the meaning of harmony.

The ancient ones devised seven forms or styles of effective meditation practices.

The Seven Basic Meditations

1. *Meditation through Breath Exercises*
   Breath is used as the tool for calming the mind and filling the body with refined chi. In a quiet state the breath is engaged consciously. The mind is told to relax on the breath, to move with the breath. As the meditation deepens, many styles of breathing are used to encourage states of wisdom and enlightenment. Qigong is an aspect of meditation through breath. This is a perfect meditation technique for anyone who longs for greater spiritual peace and yet is limited in movement. This form of meditation can be done standing or sitting. The sitting does not have to be cross-legged—one can sit Western-style in a chair. Since the integration of Qigong in the Western world, breath meditation has become a strong and viable path to spiritual

development for increasing numbers of people. This method provides access to the meditative process previously denied by the impracticability or inaccessibility of the other forms.

2. *Meditation through Concentrating All of One's Thoughts on a Single Point*
This exercise uses pinpoint mental focus to create a state in which laser-clarity becomes a way of perceiving. Directed and highly disciplined, this meditation requires a predictable structure and great mental focus. From this form of meditation one can learn the great advantage of being able to totally direct one's thoughts toward creating a desired outcome. This meditation is best done in conjunction with heart-expanding exercises to maintain the balance between head and heart.

3. *Meditation through Visuals*
This meditation can be accomplished in two ways. The first is through the act of creation. Making art and music allows a meditative state to occur when the artist and the creation become one. The second aspect is the contemplation of an art form or music, not actually creating it, but focusing entirely upon its presence. The two can also be used together. The Tibetan monks making their exquisite mandalas are in a state of deep meditation as they create with sand. The mandala itself then becomes a focus of meditation, and finally, is completely destroyed, as a reenactment of the impermanence of life.

4. *Meditation through Mantras*
This is a sound meditation, with the sound issuing from the meditator. There are words and phrases that are given great spiritual value: "Om Mani Padme Hum" is a phrase that is often used, or the word "om" is often used alone. The word "love" is used in meditation, as is the phrase "God is love." There are many. A word or a phrase is repeated in a slow, spoken repetition. The sound vibration is emphasized. This is a most ancient form of meditation and is a complex and complete path to spiritual attunement.

5. *Meditation by Absorbing the Mind in Good Will or Devotional Thoughts*
This technique uses discipline of the mind to let the will of the heart be in every waking moment. This is a good meditation for busy people because it can be carried along into life. It is the path of the saint who serves entirely

Guideline for movement meditation:
- Relax
- Know emptiness and fullness
- Have slowness and evenness
- Balance
- Root and sink
- Breathe
- Concentrate

by delving deeply into life and real people rather than withdrawing from normal life.

6. *Meditation by Identifying the Mind Essence*
   This technique identifies refined levels of the mind. It is a highly skilled form of meditation and requires a true wise teacher to help the meditator stay focused on the essence.

7. *Meditation through Movement*
   Walking, rowing, running, yoga, some Qigong, and T'ai Chi are all expressions of this style of meditation. Movement is a fully honorable form of meditation and is well suited to our busy nation. Instead of trying to sit and still the mind, the dynamic mind is instead directed. The movement is accomplished by the mind being intentionally directed into assisting with the movement. The mind is then further directed to the breath, to the chi, and finally to directing the chi intentionally. Since T'ai Chi is considered movement meditation, we'll spend a little more time exploring this form.

> Most experts agree that if we want to quiet the mind and strengthen our ability to live fully in the present, meditation is the most effective practice.
> —Fernando Raynolds

The ancient masters sought movement meditation to more effectively understand and then engage life based on the belief that we are seeking a balance where the mind directs us and the body supports us and so that a pleasurable union is formed. Normally, our thoughts are in charge of us, unless the body begins to give us trouble; then, usually with great resentment, we give some time to the body. Ideally we can learn to control and balance this relationship.

Since ninety-nine percent of our thoughts have to do with the past or the future, our thought state is not stable. Instead we have thoughts that bounce here and there, never steady, never present. It is this bouncing that keeps us from presence and appropriate response. We feel pressed upon by thoughts of events past or events yet to come, or fantasies of events occurring someplace else. It is this that prevents us from pure, clear reaction. When pure, clear reaction does occur, it is usually from the habit nature instead of the true nature.

All this is deeply difficult for the body, which carries all these bouncing feelings generated by bouncing thoughts. Yet we seldom include a behavior that directly expresses our thoughts and feelings through body action. This produces a state of consistent stress. Some stress is necessary for the body to function, but shortness of breath, fatigue, and squeamish stomach are signs of too much stress. This tension denies the proper absorption of chi.

Meditation as movement stabilizes the thoughts. This, in turn, brings order to the feelings. Immediately the body's energies start to rise with less feeling-debris flowing through. The scattered state of life led by most begins to dissolve. The movement requires complete involvement. The simplicity of the intent frees the body from aging stress, and youthful chi begins to flow freely again.

In addition to dealing with our thoughts, most of our daily life is involved with the body quietly carrying the mind from one activity to another. We expect our bodies to do this with no back talk. For instance, we relax by reading, watching TV, or going to a movie. Our minds race into the portrayed experience and the body is filled with a mass of feelings that have nothing to do with true reality. The mind has a great time escaping, but the body is now loaded up with unreleased feelings, responses, and reactions. The mind is relaxed, but the body has not been released and relaxed. This repeats throughout the day in many, many ways, a dominance of the mind and expected supportive passivity from the body. But the body does have its own life, and when the life of the body is not honored, accepted, and served, illness and early aging occur. When the body and mind are consistently not partnered in creative expression, the body takes the hit. Trouble sleeping, irritation, unexpected sadness, concern for security, questions of feeling included, and aches and pains from stress are frequent symptoms of the body's struggles.

Relaxing by doing something that combines the two pleasurably can help—this is where movement meditation comes in. Gardening and cooking are useful breaks. Do activities where the body and mind are united, where the body is obeying the will of the mind in ways that bring it pleasure. These types of relaxation are those that bring essential relaxation and joy as maturing occurs. The types of activities that the body enjoys has to do with food, nurturing, acceptance, and beauty—body and life sustaining activities.

Meditation for T'ai Chi

Meditation practices specific to T'ai Chi are woven into doing T'ai Chi. This is accomplished by directing the mind to the chi. In this way, knowledge of chi, its

When you observe nature and look at rocks and waves, you realize that each has its own nature. The wave is being wave and the rock is being rock. When the wave and the rock come together, they create rock/wave, wave/rock. They have a separateness and also a togetherness in which each one is very much itself. If the wind comes blowing and the tree is there, rooted down, then it becomes wind/tree, tree/branch/wind. Human beings can move like all these things. We can be rooted down like a rock or a tree or we can move like wind, like water.

—Al Huang

value, and what can be accomplished by coming into a deep understanding of it become clear. This clarity comes as a part of a process. The first step is usually the rather stunning realization that chi does indeed exist, that the concept of chi is not merely a fantasy of people back in a time when life and nature was seemingly often out of control and as a result the idea of chi was formed not from reality but from the need to have influence and control.

The following are T'ai Chi postures that have been classically utilized for meditation. The first one will give you the foundation you need to embrace the others as you progress through T'ai Chi, Qigong, and these meditations.

Beginning Meditation

The ideal with this initial meditation stance is to work up to twenty or thirty minutes. But just a few minutes at the beginning, particularly if you have annoying muscle holding, is a great start. Start with a few minutes, add in a few more over time, until you have finally found that twenty to thirty minutes is just right for you. This may be hard to imagine now, but when this meditation has been given its place in your life, it will become as important to you as a meal. Remember, T'ai Chi adjusts itself to you. You do it in your own rhythm and timing. Do it daily and you will never, ever regret it.

The full description of this meditation follows.

- Keep your breath easy and natural and through your nose.
- Your lips are soft, jaw relaxed back and then down. (This is the only way to release the enormous tension carried in the jaw. If it is hard to release the jaw, just do it slowly and let it become softer and softer in the mandible joint.) Your mouth may hang open a bit.
- Your head is suspended from a string, drawing both the head and the spine up, contributing to the feeling of lightness in the upper body.
- Your shoulders are loose and lowering, but not curling over the chest. Letting the head be lifted by the string helps with this.
- Your chest is soft, not inflated up or hollow. Think soft.

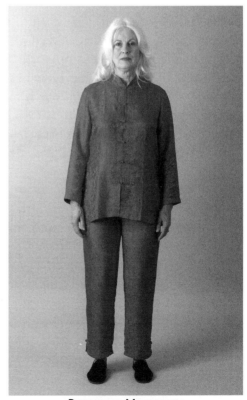

BEGINNING MEDITATION

- The base of the spine is down and you can feel the lovely tail dragging on the floor.
- As the base of the spine moves down and into place, the abdomen relaxes. The abdomen is soft, rounded, and moving naturally with the breath.
- Your arms are hanging naturally at your sides, with your elbows loose.
- Your palms are facing back.
- Your knees are soft.
- Legs are straight.
- Feet deep into molding sand.
- Your joints are open all up and down your body. Put your tongue on the upper palate.
- Let your eyes gaze ahead, find a pleasant point on which to rest your slightly unfocused gaze.
- Place your mind within your stance.
- Focus on your stable stance, your uplifted head, your shoulders moving down, the gentle wave of breath and movement in your abdomen.
- As you achieve success in this meditation, you will feel more and more comfortable. It will become a pleasure to do and one day you will feel the chi moving within you. That perception will open your life to a wonderful world of youth and vitality. This beginning meditation is hun-yuan kung in Chinese, meaning the beginning position.

Single Whip Meditation

This meditation is particularly good for the joints. It expands the joints and facilitates the movement of pre-birth chi throughout the body. By assuming the right form in a Single Whip (your teacher is essential here) seventy percent of your weight is shifted onto your left leg. As always, be sure the knee doesn't extend beyond your toes. Your eyes are focused on your left hand and your right hand is extended to the back. This is a more complex standing meditation than the first one, so do it under the wise and watchful eye of your chosen teacher.

Walking Meditation

Walking meditation is a profound and relatively simple form of focusing your meditative mind. It is, of course, a moving meditation and shares in common with all the other moving meditations focusing the mind to move chi while the body is moving. The steps for the moving meditation are found in the warm-up section, chapter 10. The primary walking meditation is moving as outlined in the instruction and photos.

The focus that provides the fertile environment for meditation and chi direction is the filling and emptying of the legs. When you imagine the solid leg becoming heavy, you are directing chi into the leg. It is this mental command

and follow-through that moves the chi according to your will. It is the constant focus on this that constitutes the meditation.

- Left leg and foot stable and heavy.
- Right leg and foot light and empty.
- Left leg and foot provides the root.
- Right leg and foot, empty, slide forward.
- Chi begins to spill from the heavy left leg and foot into the previously empty right leg and foot.
- The right leg and foot receive the chi, more and more of it. The left leg and foot have less and less and as a result are emptier and emptier.
- Right leg is now filled with chi.
- Left leg, empty and light, slides forward into a step.

Many things are accomplished with this focused, moving state. You get to become familiar with mentally directing chi. You do empty and full in orderly sequences, which assists T'ai Chi. You get to do the seventy percent-thirty percent and the thirty percent-seventy percent stance. The balanced position in the step takes place when the pelvis is directly in the middle of each foot, balanced and strong with the weight mostly (seventy percent) on one leg and less weight (thirty percent) on the other. It will help enormously with balance. It will help with refocusing efforts. It will encourage greater awareness of your tan t'ien and its source of strength for you. It teaches you to relax, relax, relax within the form. It allows you to walk in a slower, regular step instead of racing from here to there. Once you learn it, you won't be walking at a snail's pace. You can easily pace at your normal walk. Once you have integrated this, you will wonder how you ever managed without it. It will center, calm, deepen your breath, and bring you present every single time.

There are ways in which you can progress and deepen this meditation, but they should be done only when you are smooth and comfortable with the walking meditation. Here are five ways to gradually deepen this meditation experience.

1. Add the string pulling up your head. This lightens the head, lifts the step, and most importantly, lifts the spine from bottom to top. It is the lifting from the top of the head that produces lightness in the body and an opening of the all-important waist. The walking meditation, then, continues as before except now you add the third focus. You demand that the cord of chi entering your head lift up the head as it enters. You are making sure this essential flow of light, universal chi does both the jobs it is meant to do. It brings lightness. It enters the upper body through the top of the head, bringing lightness to the neck, arms, and torso. And it lifts the entire torso gently up to increase the sense of lightness and pliability.

2. Let your upper chest become so light it actually empties and becomes hollow. This step cannot be successfully achieved until step one has become familiar. You need to get the chi moving and balanced. Then the head lifts and lightens. The chi can then move and redistribute itself freely enough that this all-important sense of an empty or hollow chest seems a comfortable next step.

3. Now adjust by relaxing the shoulders. The shoulder chi feeling is the length of the shoulder between the spine and the tip of the shoulder. The awareness of the length allows the shoulder to sink without curving or arching. Bringing a dual awareness to the elbows assists with this sinking down into the lightness of your being. The elbows are also sinking. Like a gentle floating downward in water—shoulders and elbows gently, easily sink as you walk: full-empty, seventy percent-thirty percent; full-empty, seventy percent-thirty percent; full-empty, seventy percent-thirty percent.

4. Placement of the pelvis: This is an interesting and quite useful realignment of the pelvis to facilitate a smooth and balanced walk. The mind directs the chi to create a feeling of focus on your calves. So the full-empty, seventy percent-thirty percent is directed in and from the calves. Add to this direction to give a feeling of rounded space between the legs. This space permits the pelvis to reposition itself. This is accomplished by dropping the tailbone, letting it sink down and in. The focus for the walk is in the calves. The legs have a rounded space between them, and the dropped tailbone directs the pelvis slightly forward. When the walking meditation becomes familiar, you will feel a slight shifting in the pelvic floor and hips as you walk. As you swing the foot forward, the forward movement will actually come from the pelvis. So at this point, the pelvis tips forward just a bit and generating the movement of the empty leg. As the foot finds its resting place, just as the seventy percent-thirty percent is starting, the pelvis releases, tips back ever so slightly to then again tip forward as the next empty leg and foot swing or slide forward.

5. As the walk begins to free up, becoming lighter and very well balanced, it is very centering (and this really helps with directing chi movement from the tan t'ien). Imagine your tailbone is dropped down and in, in such a way that it actually hammocks the tan t'ien. When these two centers are aligned and balanced, enormous strength and stability are the normal, everyday way of life. The walking meditations culminate with a total and complete focus on the tan t'ien. The walker is free to do this because all of the previous steps to achieve this state of perfect focus are in place. Follow the wisdom of those who have gone before you. Don't do the sequential steps out of alignment. Each one, when mastered, supports the next until, like blocks

beautifully balanced on one another, they all work together so that the base block, the tan t'ien, is free to do its job of complete support.

As you progress in these meditation techniques, you may also be progressing in your T'ai Chi session. You will find a very pleasant mutual exchange occurring within you between the T'ai Chi and the meditation movement. One will bring the other into changing perspectives and a better ability to succeed as you want to. In very real but different ways, each one of these techniques accomplishes the same thing: the nurturing and refining of chi to promote excellent health and youthful well-being.

Taoist Meditations

T'ai Chi, being a part of Taoism, also uses techniques for meditation that are based in Taoist techniques. These techniques do not, however, challenge or compete with any faith. These techniques extend into the common ground that connects all faiths—compassion, love, understanding, and concern for humankind's well-being. Your faith, whatever it is, will be enhanced by the tools learned in T'ai Chi and Qigong. You will not feel compelled to turn from your own beliefs. These techniques improve each person, which, in turn, improves each person's ability to be more present and involved with their own faith.

The standing meditation is a cornerstone of Taoist, and therefore T'ai Chi, meditation. The Chinese term for this form of meditation is *jan-chung*, or Stand as a Stake. This is a very interesting meditation. It will make immediately obvious where in your body your unnecessary tension resides. To stand steady, unmoving, is not as simple as it may sound, and there is no better way to get to the root of your holding and blocking of chi through muscle tension.

To achieve this meditation posture requires a blend of mind and body. Use your mind to create the images that help the body pose into this unmoving form. For instance, use your mind to adapt the feet to the best way to support this meditation. Let your mind guide the feet to touch the ground gently, softly, like settling into warm, wet sand. The feet settle into the sand and the substance of the sand supports the feet. It is this feeling of support that allows the next step to occur. As your feet take on the full weight of your body, guide them mentally to feel as if they are sinking down easily into the sand, the ground, and finally to the center of the earth. (This center is warm, not molten.) This allows the feet to open and receive the gift of earth chi. This chi fills the feet and legs, and the body becomes supported by its energizing and balancing influence. It is this earth energy that enables the lower half of the body to become as solid and stable as a mountain. But interestingly, this very real feeling of absolute solidity is permeated with the recognition of total connection. Another great paradox. Completely solid and boundaried in the lower body and completely connected through contained receptivity. This in itself is a primary T'ai Chi standing meditation. Feet down into earth, rooted gently, and yielding, receiving earth's chi and simply letting the lower body fill and become more and more solid. As the lower body develops its solidity, the upper body—another paradox—becomes lighter and lighter. As you become more familiar and therefore more accomplished with this energetic reality, your lower half might feel solid while it might feel as if the wind is blowing through the cells of your upper half.

This meditation will call to your attention areas of tension within your body that no longer understand the concept of release and relax. These areas will begin to make their presence felt. Aching, itching, and soreness are common. When the tense areas inevitably call to you, use the draining sand technique. Relax them down, let them go, use your mind to create an image of the tension becoming sand and draining down, out of the troubled area, down to the ground, sand going on down to the center of the earth to where the feet stand. Allow the entire body to be filled with the image of sand draining down allowing all the muscles, from your toes to the crown of your head, and everything in between, to become free and light. The lower body will also feel free and light. This is because the feeling of stability doesn't come from holding the hips, thighs, calves, ankles, and feet solid. It comes from releasing the tension in the hips, thighs, calves, ankles, and feet, and allowing your lower body to receive the chi from earth, which is solid in its nature. Another dichotomy, as the lower body releases tension, becoming freer and pliable, it also becomes more solid, steady, and foundational. When the lower body is filled with earth chi, the upper body fills with chi from heaven. As the dense stress and strain releases from the head, neck, shoulders, arms, hands, torso, and waist, the chi from the sky, the universe, heaven, flows in. It is this mutual opening to earth and heaven that creates within the T'ai Chi body stability and lightness. The most wonderful part is that to achieve this, one must only be soft and receptive. This is the training of the T'ai Chi meditation to join mind and body to be available to these two essential life-giving flows of chi. This is the foundation for them cultivating, refining, and directing chi. Only when both flows of chi in the body are where they are supposed to be can this be accomplished. The waist is the merging ground. It is for this reason the waist is always kept open, flexible, and moving in T'ai Chi. When someone has too much heavenly chi beneath the waist, the person is ungrounded and unable to build a solid life that expresses them and serves them simultaneously. If a person has too much earth chi in the upper body, they are plodding and practical to the point of no vision, no inspiration, and no real joy. By incorporating this very simple meditation, your chi flows will correct and you will be off and running into a more youthful and healthy experience.

It is usually advised to practice meditation dovetailed with Qigong two or three times a day. If this regimen is consistent, the result will be the precious prebirth chi, the chi cultivated in Qigong, which will fill and spill out of the tan t'ien. It is this spillway of chi that becomes free for direction. To someone who has arrived at this point, the breath will couple with the chi and create gentle waves of life, strength, and youth rising and returning in the lower half of the body. It is not really possible to accurately describe the feeling of timeless youth, vitality, and personal potency this facilitates, but it is worth taking the time to do the meditation of your choice and couple it with Qigong practice. The abdomen becomes so filled with the waves of youth and vitality that the ancient Chinese called this experience *chi-hai*, or the ocean of chi. This stage of chi development creates an abdomen that is soft and supple. This pliability is the sign that great vitality has become a fact of life. It is at this point that meditation takes on a new and vital importance. With chi filling the abdomen and moving in waves of youth within, it is now available for direction. The first step is to train the mind to direct the chi throughout the body in a manner so thorough that the entire body is now filled with vital and balanced chi.

Again, no words can adequately convey the deep renaissance that becomes available. To achieve this state of youthful health requires a commitment, but the path has been so well laid out by those before us that it is a simple task, a task that requires only the personal discipline to do it. It is the understanding of these basic methods and principles that create success in one's own personal energetic practices. Your own experience is what gives you the essential data to further your experiment with creating a vastly improved vitality and self-awareness. The principles teach how to develop your personal physical and mental abilities in gentle accordance with your meditative practices. It is this commitment that allows a personal experience of chi to emerge, and once this milestone has been passed, many wonderful things occur. Health, vitality, wisdom, and greatly improved self-awareness lead each and every practitioner into a world of understanding. Simple to write, amazing, and yet completely ordinary to experience. This elevation of the self is the oddest of all dichotomies. Life becomes exquisite and a great gift, while simultaneously, the absolute ordinary rhythm of life is found.

Setting the Mood

The quality of energy we generate through out Qigong and T'ai Chi practice is strongly impacted by the mood or mindset we adopt in our practice. These arts can be practiced to develop martial art skills, to gain health, or for personal and spiritual growth. If your focus is martial, then your attention should be on power and sensitivity and the mood should be one of indomitable determination. On the other hand, health and personal development are best promoted through a mood that is as uplifting, inspiring, and energizing as possible.

Ultimately, this is an individual recipe, but may well include elements of internally and externally directed compassion and acceptance, gentleness, openness, vitality, humor, and lightness. One important feature of this is to cultivate the habit of smiling. By physically smiling, we create the foundation of the uplifting state we seek in our practice.

—Fernando Raynolds

Chapter 14

T'ai Chi and Sexuality

Each person is different, and this difference bears within it the requirement of self-knowledge. It is through knowledge of individual qualities—physical, emotional, spiritual, and mental—that the wise distribution of personal chi can occur. Some of this personal distribution is achieved by simply learning T'ai Chi and Qigong and allowing the chi to store, balance, and refine within throughout the movements. The other distribution is to specifically direct chi through the body to a specific area or organ of weakness to strengthen it. This focused direction can be done mentally through the focused blending of mind and breath. Both of these relationships to chi can be accomplished in the sexual arena as well.

This internal peace, maintained at all times, was the goal of the martial arts school. In self-mastery through discipline, this internal state was developed and maintained, sometimes in extraordinary circumstances. Ancient Chinese warriors applied the carefully crafted self-discipline to draw chi through every area of life—martial arts, communication, art, gardening, eating, meditation, and sex. Becoming more and more peaceful, these men could stride forth into battle and be the perfect warrior, refining the base but abundant chi that surrounded him in the horror of war for his own improvement and evolution. Unwilling to be overwhelmed by hatred, lust, frenzied killing, or overwhelming fear, these warriors knew how to take this intensely abundant chi pattern and use it for their own. Their discipline led to an astonishing ability to master their relationship to chi and their own personal inner development.

War provided an intense environment for the commingling of chi. Chi interaction happens as soon as two people, and their two chi fields, meet. Sex provided the other commingling environment that could match and exceed the intense environment of war, and it provided the balanced opposite experience. Destruction on the one hand, creation on the other. This produced the goal to remain, as in war, deeply connected and utterly contained—fully present, fully engaged, and completely involved in self-refinement.

All the self-containment of war found its opposite in the bedroom. Here the warrior found a new world of commingling chi and an opportunity for refinement through attraction to and need for the partner.

Commingling of chi fields occurs as soon as communication starts and intensifies if the chi boundary becomes soft and permeable. At this point the chi mingling that continues is the beginning of intimacy. Commingling chi creates intimacy in the four areas of development: mind melding, emotional oneness, spiritual upliftment, and physical ecstasy. The chi boundary is most open at physical ecstasy when the chi is refined and moved through the other three areas. This happens in two arenas: love and abuse. One melts the boundaries, the other destroys them. One is a true commingling that creates self-confidence and good will, the other an assault that destroys, along with the boundaries, a confident, contained self and sense of trust. To have suffered abuse makes the need to embrace the path of self-knowledge even more imperative. Through T'ai Chi and Qigong, the infusion of low vibrating chi that is a part of abuse can be elevated within the abused individual. This is the path to true inner freedom and acceptance. The commingling that produces the most refined and therefore sweetest chi was believed to be offered in one environment alone—sex.

The transmission of chi through touch was the basis for T'ai Chi Ch'uan teachings on sexuality and right behavior. Of course, because we're talking about Chinese martial art masters here, the goal was to develop self-mastery in this arena of human life. The goal was to form a sexual union that would bring both partners to T'ai Chi as it expressed Wu Chi, the moment of life initiating life. As the chi flowed and mingled, yin and yang would divide between each partner. Each one would become one-half of the whole. The other would become the perfect other half. In this union regarded as perfect, the discipline that was applied was designed to arrive at higher and higher levels of refined bliss and ecstasy.

When two who are attracted to each other meet, chi begins to flow back and forth. As the mutual physical attraction increases, the chi will circulate ever faster. When attraction increases to arousal, the chi has reached a point of great momentum. This momentum creates intense and usually compelling magnetic attraction that cannot be denied.

There is a teaching in the Vedic tradition that claims the universe was born from pure sound. And in Genesis from the Bible: "And the sound was made word."

T'ai Chi Ch'uan's teachings about this potential union were clear and there were precise ways to enhance sexual union. This approach would ensure that both partners would have a life-enhancing, spiritually-enhancing experience. The core of this is the foundational belief that all of life's journey is provided for one reason alone: to continually store, cultivate, and refine chi so that one is able to constantly incorporate, transcend, and supercede each experience life presents. The exquisite union with another offered rarified commingling and a unique opportunity to be filled with bliss and humility simultaneously. This most exalted union was deemed critical in intent, process, and outcome. Calm control and mastery of self, in both partners, was the key. Expressed incorrectly, the commingling of the chi would drain vitality and health from both, thus producing anxiety and frustration.

> Human beings are of such a nature that they should have not only material facilities, but spiritual sustenance as well. Without spiritual sustenance it is difficult to get and maintain peace of mind.
> —Dalai Lama

Chi is a perfect concentration in the egg/yin and the sperm/yang. As the commingling chi between partners intensifies, the concentrated chi in the egg and sperm join in an energetic dance of life and regeneration. As this dance of yin and yang intensifies further, the partners move closer and closer to fulfillment. The moment of fulfillment is the culmination of the level of refinement gained within this chi dance of life.

From close examination of the principles of chi and sex, guidelines were developed. The egg is internal within the woman, always within her eternally connecting her to creative life. She was encouraged to experience fulfillment to nourish this eternal chi life. This gave her more rejuvenating chi for her own spiritual benefit. She then enriched her partner by commingling this chi connected to eternal life. Both became connected to life through her body. Both she and her partner sought this goal.

Males were encouraged to release only when wanting to produce a child. When a man released, his source of refined, rejuvenating chi was given to the woman and this added up to a loss of life-sustaining chi for the man. This loss of chi was taken very, very seriously. Men were taught to develop sexual mastery over release or counseled to be celibate. The man was given tools to enable him to engage his partner for longer and longer periods of time. Sensuality and sexuality combined and produced a calm mind, a state of inner relaxation, and a deep sense of commingling chi for a union of love. Release was not the sought-after culmination. This was replaced by a heightened sense of sexual refinement and spiritual pleasure. This then defined a different type of fulfillment. Freed from easing tension through release, a new and valuable experience could emerge. The commingling chi, enhanced by the woman's fulfillment, would heighten to a point where bliss was an ongoing, not momentary, state.

Sexual arts became a central part of the Taoist philosophy of wholeness emerging through chi. A circle of life in which all was connected and all affected, nothing was separate or isolated and sexual arts became the living embodiment of this truth of life.

Different sexual positions became a part of this erotic world. Positions prescribed to enhance the health and well-being of specific organs. Breath was seen as a two-part activity. Breath to the lungs and chi to the tan t'ien and dispersal. Sex was similar. First that all-so-human attraction and arousal, and then specific positions used to drive the chi more deeply into a depleted organ.

Shallow, casual, or abusive sex was eschewed. Not only was it not helpful, but the chi that was engaged in the experiences was the opposite of heightened awareness. Instead it was fraught with long-term peril because of the dangerously low vibrating chi and the negative focus that aligned with it.

The absolute ideal was to have partners committed to their own development, passionately finding bliss of union with each other and then refining their intimacy over time. With both partners relaxed and mutually sustaining, an environment of spiritual development emerged. This became the chi spring for a multifaceted, satisfying union, and a profound spiritual awareness.

Frequently Asked Questions

How long will it take to learn T'ai Chi?

A timeless question. You can begin to develop the body memory after about six to eight weeks, or forty-two to fifty-six days. This would include a primary learning time, a class, a video, a book, or a TV class as a resource and then doing T'ai Chi each day. It is this combination of learning a new movement and then repeating it in the ensuing days that builds up the memory of the movement in the muscle fibers. This six-to-eight-week time period is the reason why most beginning classes are arranged to be precisely this length. This, of course, doesn't mean you will have T'ai Chi down pat, but you will be starting to feel more comfortable. You may also start feeling the beginning of its benefits.

What length of time is best for daily learning?

Depending not on the free time available, but on your energy level, practice from ten to thirty minutes each day. This length of time will allow the entire short form to become, over time, very much yours.

How long does the learning go on?

This really depends on how far you decide to take it. Are you doing T'ai Chi for specific benefits? Do you have a clear goal? The attainment of the benefits and/or the goal may define the length of time you want to be learning. After reaching these preset points of success, you may decide to simply settle into the form at this level of learning. Doing T'ai Chi each day in a way that is fine for you and with you is a clear success.

You may also find yourself interested in a longer learning time. It may come as a surprise that you do want to explore more closely the nuances in the form. T'ai Chi is like any art form—the more you do it, the deeper and richer it becomes for you. You may in the end make it a lifelong dedication to learning from teachers and/or a lifelong dedication to learning from the form alone as you repeat the patterns of movement. T'ai Chi will join you wherever you are and it will serve you however you do it. You just simply need to do T'ai Chi to do it.

What are the benefits of T'ai Chi?

The research is still being done in the field of Western science. The value of T'ai Chi from this perspective is fledgling but bountiful. First and foremost T'ai Chi assists balance. There is an abundance of research that confirms T'ai Chi improves balance and reduces falls in elderly T'ai Chi practitioners, because of the graceful, moving emphasis on the full and empty legs as well as the seventy percent-thirty percent stances. It dramatically improves coordination because while both sides of the body are moving and flowing together, they are doing different things. This creates an opportunity for the wiring in the brain to become more alert. The outcome is greatly improved coordination. T'ai Chi's rhythmic movement creates an internal environment of relaxed comfort even when the outer environment is filled with stressful action. T'ai Chi improves posture, which in turn creates a world of valuable side effects. The lungs open and breath is easier and fuller. The spine straightens, giving the torso the upright support it needs for the organs to have the circulation and space they need for healthy functioning. Walking becomes effortless as the muscles begin to line up and function properly. Each muscle group does its correct movement and in doing so supports the others to do the same. Breath control is a very big plus. To have full breath means oxygen and chi are nourishing the brain, organs, skin, etc. as needed for functioning. Increased flexibility becomes another byproduct of adequate breathing and properly executed T'ai Chi. This is muscle flexibility and amazing joint flexibility as well. Just make sure you keep your steps in the form small so your weight-bearing knee is always under you, not way out from your torso in a big step out. T'ai Chi has been reported to help hypertension, headaches, improve depression, and improve skin, as well as stabilizing weight.

If you have a health concern, be sure to let your doctor know you are thinking of learning T'ai Chi. The advice you get will be essential to your health maintenance.

T'ai Chi also facilitates the accumulation, storage, and refinement of our life force, chi. It is this rare and remarkable skill that gives T'ai Chi the ability to be more than an exercise. It is this relationship to chi that has given rise to the ancient reverential claims of T'ai Chi's stunning ability to slow aging and improve vitality well into the elder years. These claims, as yet uncorroborated by science, still reverberate throughout T'ai Chi classrooms the world over. If you stick with doing T'ai Chi, your own personal list of rewards and benefits will grow.

What is Qigong?

Qigong is more ancient than T'ai Chi. In China, Qigong dates back to prehistoric times. The general belief is about 3,000 years. It does appear that Qigong developed a very long time ago and has been done by many, many people over time. Qigong is a Western approach to Chi Kung (Chi meaning vitality and Kung meaning force). Qigong, or Chi Kung, means vital force or developing one's internal force. Qigong is the internal force, and T'ai Chi is mastering the external force. Qigong is devoted entirely to breath expansion and control. In the classic Qigong, the legs are rooted, the arms move in specific synchrony with the breath. Qigong draws in, fills up, and then sets forth to deliberately cultivate chi, the vital force. Because the movements are much simpler than T'ai Chi and there is a great compatibility between them, many T'ai Chi instructors recommend that people who are insecure with T'ai Chi start with Qigong. It can be, and has always been, done on its own. If anything, T'ai Chi Ch'uan probably incorporated it. Qigong is a force for health, vitality, and increased well-being. It is easy to learn and can be learned very easily from a book.

What if T'ai Chi doesn't work for me?

There are different strokes for different folks, no doubt. T'ai Chi, though amazing for millions, is not everyone's cup of tea. If you have tried it, given it your six to eight weeks and once a day doing, and it hasn't clicked, then switch over to Qigong. The benefits are similar. T'ai Chi provides more because of the complexity of the movement, but Qigong provides an enormous amount of benefit, certainly enough to satisfy the most demanding student.

What does one wear for T'ai Chi and Qigong?

Lightweight clothes to move in that allow you breathe easily. Clothes that permit free and easy movement—a comfortable, expandable waistband, plenty of room for the shoulders and knees for stretching and bending. Lightweight for temperature comfort. The most important thing in T'ai Chi and Qigong attire is the shoes. These must be made of cloth with rubber soles that bring ample stability to your feet. The shoes have no support, so if you need a heel or arch support, check with the appropriate doctor to get the right flexible fit that gives you comfort and the ability to move your feet around on the floor.

What if my T'ai Chi teachers are limited and I love T'ai Chi but don't like the teacher?

Lucky you! This is a perfect time to learn the craft and to see your teacher only as a tool to get to where you want to go. This actually can simplify the student-teacher relationship, which unless stopped, can become a bit follower-like. This attitude impairs one's satisfactory relationship to T'ai Chi by making the instructor the focus rather than keeping T'ai Chi the focus. The instructor is the vehicle.

What is the best learner's attitude for T'ai Chi and Qigong?

The Chinese hold their ancestors in reverence. They appreciate them daily for being the ones who have gone before and have left such a rich legacy for their progeny. This is a natural and useful learning attitude for T'ai Chi and Qigong, a recognition that this elegant movement has been crafted by the moving bodies of thousands before you. You are stepping into a form. Open to your instruction recognizing that this probably won't be the easiest movement you have ever learned, but it may well be the most valuable. Be willing to be corrected. Embrace doing it daily. Be open to how T'ai Chi and Qigong affect your life.

I have some movement impairment. Can T'ai Chi and Qigong work for me?

Yes, absolutely. Be comfortable about modifying it as you need to facilitate your comfort in learning the movement your own way! Because you are essentially working with chi, you can do empty and full legs while sitting, even if you can't use your legs at all. Just imagine one full and heavy and one light and airy. Then move the rest of you as best you can.

If you have a challenge, like dyslexia, T'ai Chi can help your wiring sort itself out a bit. Your dyslexic moments may begin to reduce in number and length.

With my youth now in the past, what of my youthfulness will I get back with T'ai Chi and Qigong?

First and foremost, you will have more energy. You will become and feel more lithe and graceful. Your ease of movement, from simple sitting to dancing, will increase. Your girth will begin to pare down, particularly if you eventually learn the full yang form. Your all-over muscle tone will improve. Your skin tone will brighten. Your sense of security with yourself will be more confident. Your life and the future will seem brighter. Your sense of stress will diminish and your sense of pleasure will constantly increase.

How can T'ai Chi and Qigong help me with life's challenges?

It is true that the last half of life is filled with more loss than the first half of life. In our culture we like to pretend it is a mistake to have loss and that if we live right, are good people, and mind our p's and q's, we won't ever experience it. This is Western lack of realism. We all need tools to integrate life's challenges, loss being a very big challenge when it occurs. Loss is a natural part of life. T'ai Chi and Qigong are natural purveyors of life. To have access to this dance of life in the face of loss produces inner equanimity. The loss is not reduced, but the tools for going on are inborn in your T'ai Chi and Qigong form.

Is T'ai Chi a faith? Will it compete with or be incompatible with my faith and religion?

T'ai Chi is a movement and philosophy. It is not a faith. It is an ancient tool for profound health and well-being. It supports any faith by improving life quality and connection. It does not demand obedience to a belief.

Will T'ai Chi and Qigong enhance my spiritual development?

Yes indeed. This is the ultimate function of both T'ai Chi and Qigong, to engage the participant into the chi in a way that harmony, inner peace, and resiliency reside within. These qualities deepen as the form is further explored over time.

When and where do I do T'ai Chi?

Classically T'ai Chi and Qigong are both done in the morning, outside, moving barefoot over the morning dew. The air is the freshest and the day awaits. So if you can do this, with shoes if you prefer, that is probably the ideal. However, it is well within the practical realm that you will have to carve a time space out of an already full life. In this case, pick a time that seems like a reasonable candidate. Then commit to it. Push back your life. Dedicate yourself to doing T'ai Chi for the length of time you have predetermined. You can experiment with times too. Some find T'ai Chi before bed relaxes them. Others find it wakes them up. Some do T'ai Chi in the middle of the afternoon to bridge that low time. Others prefer to do it before a meal to quell a generous appetite. Before a stressful event is a good time to insert T'ai Chi. Pick your time with the wisdom of self-knowledge and then just do it.

The question of where to do it is a great one, because the answer is so filled with variety. Do it where you want, and on a regular basis. It is great to have a T'ai Chi space that seems comparatively peaceful and quiet. You can also insert T'ai Chi whenever you want its gift. It requires a relatively small space and needs nothing more than you, so it can be taken with you easily and done anywhere. Your only mitigating factor may be self-consciousness.

Can T'ai Chi improve my memory?

Oh yes, memory. The problem with memory can certainly show up when trying to learn all the this-ways and that-ways of T'ai Chi. T'ai Chi will definitely improve your patience, that's for sure. And then there is memory. T'ai Chi will challenge memory and it will also encourage your nervous system to rev it up. To the degree that keeping the body and mind active keep youthfulness, T'ai Chi will actively contribute to that end. It certainly won't make memory worse and it might very well help.

Can I use T'ai Chi for self-protection?

T'ai Chi Ch'uan, with the fist added in, is perfectly suitable for self-protection. When the Ch'uan is removed, leaving T'ai Chi, the movement becomes oriented toward health, well-being, and balance. What will help in self-protection is that lithe movement, and balance improves so very much. The T'ai Chi can make it easier to fit into a self-protection class. Also, T'ai Chi can improve intuition, which, if you pay attention, can keep you from heading into bad places.

What are the right questions for tracking down a perfect instructor?

Glance through chapter 5. The guidelines for this are pretty straightforward.

Are there other books recommended for further reading?

The resource area of this book is filled with ideas for great books on T'ai Chi, Qigong, and related subjects.

Is T'ai Chi just a reduced and diminished T'ai Chi Ch'uan?

There are certainly Tai Chi Ch'uan teachers who feel T'ai Chi is a poor excuse for what the ancient masters were transmitting. There are, as well many, many people whose lives have been changed by T'ai Chi. These people will say to a person T'ai Chi is not a reduced anything, but a gift to anyone who takes the time to learn it.

Can T'ai Chi help me with my stress level?

Yes, absolutely. Do it, and your stress will drop and you will see an improvement in the problems you have that stem from stress. Tell your doctor what you are doing and monitor your progress.

Will T'ai Chi improve my looks?

The best look in the world is the healthy look. There is no surgery, lotion, or pill that can give you true health and the look that goes with it. But both T'ai Chi and Qigong will bring your health into bloom, perhaps full bloom. And that will help you look terrific.

Will T'ai Chi improve my sex life?

T'ai Chi and Qigong are both, first and foremost, involved with enhancing, redistributing, and balancing vitality, or chi. The rebalance, coupled with learning how to focus chi, can help enhance sex from first glance to post-orgasm tremendously. This can then be expanded by utilizing the tantra aspects of T'ai Chi. Positions, breath control, and relaxation techniques become potent tools for improving sensuality and sexuality.

What might T'ai Chi lead me to philosophically?

T'ai Chi and Qigong's access to chi is the central bubbling spring for the entire fertile terrain of Chinese medicine. It is very likely that you may choose to explore further Chinese medical beliefs and perhaps the Tao itself. These are not T'ai Chi or Qigong, however. T'ai Chi and Qigong are not a belief. They are an experience of liveliness.

What is the vision now being carried for T'ai Chi?

Great question, because T'ai Chi is in a tremendous flux. T'ai Chi is about forty years old and is a branch of T'ai Chi Ch'uan, which is two thousand years old. T'ai Chi Ch'uan is most likely born from the root of Qigong, which is at least three thousand years old. Both Qigong and T'ai Chi Ch'uan grew as the need of people directed them. In this way they are born from the people of China. It will be the same for T'ai Chi. T'ai Chi will follow the tradition and meet the people where they are and provide what we need. It looks like this may mean improving and strengthening the immune system, finding consistent inner peace within world conflicts, helping improve the last half of life as science and medicine combine to lengthen our years, appreciating nature and finding new belief in assisting her preservations. And there will be so many more. You will find your own vision as T'ai Chi and Qigong meet you as you are and help you up to the next rung.

Will T'ai Chi and Qigong improve my self-esteem and/or self-worth?

These issues are an indication of being out of alignment with one's true nature. T'ai Chi and Qigong, by correcting disturbing flows of chi, create an environment within that encourages the true, joyous inner nature to emerge and thrive.

Will I benefit from T'ai Chi or Qigong if I don't do them regularly?

Nope.

What is the difference between T'ai Chi Ch'uan and T'ai Chi?

T'ai—supreme. Chi—ultimate. Ch'uan—fist. Supreme ultimate fist. T'ai Chi Ch'uan was developed to bring warriors into peak physical, emotional, mental, and spiritual perfection for winning performances in the frequent Chinese theaters of war.

T'ai Chi—supreme ultimate with no fist—is the tool for physical, emotional, mental, and spiritual perfection without the fist. All health, well-being, and lasting vitality.

Will T'ai Chi and Qigong help me with other forms of exercise?

Yes, both help with breath, oxygenation, and stamina. And T'ai Chi helps with balance and flexibility. From running to snowshoeing, swimming to rowing, skateboarding to kayaking, they will both help.

Resources

Selected Bibliography and Recommended Books

It is surprising to see T'ai Chi and Qigong books with no bibliography of resources offered. These ancient, crafted forms emerge enhanced by many thousands. Words, wisdom, and joy in the act of T'ai Chi'ing abound. These are only a few that may enrich you. There are many, many more.

T'ai Chi References

Cassileth, Barrie. "T'ai Chi May Pay Off in Unconventional Ways," *Los Angeles Times*. February 4, 2002. S. 6.

Chen, Lam Kam. *Step by Step T'ai Chi*. New York: Fireside Books, 2003.

Chen, William C. C. *Body Mechanics of Tai Chi Chuan*. www.williamccchen.com.

Ch'ing, Chen Man. *Cheng Tzu's Thirteen Treatises on T'ai Chi Ch'uan*. Berkeley: North Atlantic Books, 1984.

Galante, Lawrence. *Tai Chi: The Supreme Ultimate*. Boston: Red Wheel, 1983.

Huang, Al. *Embrace Tiger, Return to Mountain*. Berkeley: Celestial Arts, 1988.

Jou, Tsung Hwa. *The Tao of T'ai Chi Ch'uan, Way to Rejuvenation* (also known as: *The Dao of Taijiquan)*. Scottsdale, Arizona: Tai Chi Foundation, 1991.

Kauz, Herman. *Tai Chi Handbook*. New York: Double Day, 1974.

Kit, Wong Kiew. *The Complete Book of T'ai Chi Ch'uan*. Boston: Tuttle Publishing, 2002.

Lee, Ph.D., Martin with Emily Lee, Melinda Lee, and Joyce Lee. *Restore Yourself with T'ai Chi*. New York: Sterling Publishing, 2003.

Liang, T. T. *T'ai Chi Ch'uan for Health and Self Defense*. New York: Random House, 1977.

Liao, Waysun. *The Essence of T'ai Chi*. Boston: Shambhala Publications, 2003.

Liao, Waysun, trans. *T'ai Chi Classics*. Boston: Shambhala Publications, 2001.

Lo, Benjamin Pang Jing with Robert Amacker, Martin Inn, and Susan Foe. *The Essence of T'ai Chi Ch'uan*. Berkeley: North Atlantic Books, 1979.

Lowenthall, Wolfe. There *Are No Secrets—Prof. Chen Man-Ch'ing and his T'ai Chi Ch'uan*. Berkeley: North Atlantic Books, 2003.

Olson, Stuart Alve. *T'ai Chi According to the I Ching—Embodying the Principals of the Book of Changes.* Rochester, Vermont: Inner Traditions, 2001.

Pawlett, Ray. *A Beginner's Guide to T'ai Chi.* New York: Sterling Publishing, 2001.

Smith, Robert. *T'ai Chi—Cheng Man Ching.* Boston: Tuttle Publishing, 1985.

Sun, Wei Yu with William Chen. *T'ai Chi Ch'uan: The Gentle Workout for Mind and Body.* New York: Sterpling Publishing, 1995.

Tegner, Bruce. *Kung Fu and T'ai Chi: Chinese Karate.* Thor Publishing, 1983.

Wile, Doug. *T'ai Chi Touchstones: Yang Family Secret Transmissions.* Brooklyn: Sweet Chi Press, 1983.

Yu, Tricia. *T'ai Chi Mind and Body.* New York: D.K. Publishing Inc., 2003.

Philosophy References
Bercholz, Samuel, ed. *Entering the Stream.* Boston: Shambhala Publications, 1994

Cleary, Thomas F., ed. *The Spirit of Tao.* Boston: Shambhala Publications, 1998.

Hanh, Thich Nhat. *The Miracle of Mindfulness.* New York: Riverhead Books, 1975.

Kaptchuk, Ted J. *The Web That Has No Weaver.* New York: McGraw-Hill, 2000.

Schiller, David. *Little Zen Companion.* New York: Workman, 1994.

Suzuki, Shunryu. *Not Always So: Practicing the True Spirit of Zen.* New York: HarperCollins, 2002.

Tsu, Lao, Gia Fu Feng, trans. and Jane English, trans. *Tao Te Ching.* New York: Vintage Books, 1997.

Wilhelm, Richard, trans. *I Ching, Chinese Book of Changes.* Princeton: Princeton University Press, 1971.

Qi and Health References
Eden, Donna and David Feinstein. *Energy Medicine.* New York: J. P. Tarcher, 1999.

Frantzis, Bruce Kumar. *Opening the Energy Gates of Your Body: The Tao of Energy Enhancement.* Berkeley: North Atlantic Books, 1993.

Haas, MD., Elson M. *Staying Healthy with the Seasons.* Berkeley: Celestial Arts, 1981.

Jahnke, O.M.D., Roger. *The Healing Promise of Qi: Creating Extraordinary Wellness Through Qigong and T'ai Chi.* New York: McGraw-Hill, 2002.

Body Awareness Resources
Cromptom, Paul. *Walking Meditation*. London: HarperCollins UK, 1997.

Feldenkrais, Moshu. *Awareness Through Movement*. San Francisco: Harper San Francisco, 1991.

Videos
Das, Lama Surya. *Natural Meditation*. Boulder: Sounds True, 2002.

Hooten, Clair. *The Method, T'ai Chi, Beginner Level*. Parade, 1994. 800-272-4214.

Raynolds, Fernando. *Learning T'ai Chi, Beginner Level*. nsjk@wave.net.

William, Sifu. *Cheng Man Ch'ing's T'ai Chi Ch'uan*. Patience T'ai Chi Association. www.patiencetaichi.com

Music
Todd Barton
Meditative Shakuhaci Music
1. Shakuhaci Ma, CD
   Zen meditation pieces 1.8 Shakuhaci
2. Ro, CD
   Original music for meditation
   long 2.8shakuhaci
   http://www.mp3.com/shakuhacima
3. T'ai Chi Shakuhaci, cassette tape
   www.shakuhaci.com

Sequoia Records, CDs and cassette tapes
800-524-5513
www.sequoiarecoreds.com
   Oneness—Meditation. Slow
   Music for Reiki and Meditation—Quiet, healing
   Misty Forest Morning—Etheric, Tibetan Bells, chimes
   Garden of Serenity—Indian tamboura, water birds

Journals
T'ai Chi magazine
Wayfarer Publications
800-888-9119

Subtle Energies
The International Society for the Study of Subtle Energies and Energy Medicine

Websites
Golden T'ai Chi for Seniors
www.taichiforseniors.com

T'ai Chi Productions
www.taichiproductions.com

The Tai Chi Site
www.thetaichisite.com

Easy T'ai Chi for Busy People
www.easytaichi.com

Tantra T'ai Chi
www.tantrataichi.com

Foundations
T'ai Chi Foundation
212-645-7010
www.taichifoundation.org

Green Tea
Excellent and classic green tea:
Bamboo Tea House
221 Yale Avenue
Claremont CA 91711
909-626-7668
www.bambooteas.com

Glossary

5 Elements. The basis of understanding of Chinese philosophy of health and oneness.

The Book of Changes, or *I Ching.* A book that acts as a guide for the reader as it embodies the philosophy of the Tao. E CHING

Chi. The cosmic energy flow of life. CHEE

Ch'i Kung. The use of breathing to develop the chi for special purposes, such as fighting and healing. CHEE GONG

Lao Tzu. Philosopher of Taoism.

Qigong. Breath skill. (Also spelled Chi-Kung, the traditional English spelling of the traditional Chinese characters.) KEY GONG

T'ai Chi. Supreme ultimate. TIE CHEE

T'ai Chi Ch'uan. Supreme ultimate fist. TIE CHEE CHEWAN

T'ai Chi Master. A highly skilled teacher of T'ai Chi.

Tan-t'ien. Deep in the center of the belly one and one-third inches below the navel. A place of centering yourself and a gathering place for chi. DAN T'YEN

The Tao. The Chinese philosophy of the way of Taoism. THE DAO

Wu Chi. The Great Void.

Yang. Male energy of the substantial, the hard, the movement. YANG

Yang School. The type of T'ai Chi taught in this book.

Yin. Female energy of the insubstantial, the soft, the still. YIN